FROM FARMERS BOY TO FINE WINES

THE COLOURFUL LIFE OF

GEORGE ARTHUR

MEREO

Mereo Books

2nd Floor, 6-8 Dyer Street, Cirencester, Gloucestershire, GL7 2PF
An imprint of Memoirs Book Ltd. www.mereobooks.com

From farmer's boy to fine wines: 978-1-86151-957-3

First published in Great Britain in 2020
by Mereo Books, an imprint of Memoirs Books Ltd.

The address for Memoirs Books Ltd. can be
found at www.memoirspublishing.com

Memoirs Books Ltd. Reg. No. 7834348

Typeset in 11/15pt Century Schoolbook
by Wiltshire Associates Ltd.
Printed and bound in Great Britain

CONTENTS

ACKNOWLEDGEMENTS

And thanks to people who helped me along the way:

William Hignett, my mother's brother-in-law, who bought Bleak House Farm and provided the five of us with a family home when we had no money.

Francis Montagu-James, a former director of Johnnie Walker, who put in a good word or two when I was made redundant in my early fifties.

Nigel Jagger, who gave me a job at that time – and many others too

Jill Romney, nurse and friend over many years, who came to help me deal with Patricia when there was nobody else to turn to.

The West Indian lay pastor whose kind words to Patricia when she had terminal cancer made both our lives more bearable – he was a miracle worker.

And most of all my sadly-missed wife Patricia, with whom I had a love affair for 53 years.

LIST OF EMPLOYERS

—✕—

Royal Air Force (National Service)
British Transport Commission
Dexion Ltd
The Distillers Company
Cert plc

HOMES

—✕—

Sandy Lane Farm, Knutsford, Cheshire
Lower Peover, Cheshire
Fitton Town Farm, Lower Alderley, Macclesfield
Poplar Farm, Daresbury, Cheshire
Birch Tree Farm, Onston, Northwich
Bleak House Farm, Rudheath, Northwich
After marriage:
West Road, Weaverham
Green End Road, Boxmoor, Herts
Fountain Road, Northwich, Cheshire
South End Drive, Kingswinford, West Midlands
Stratford House, Claverley, Shropshire
Thame, Oxfordshire

PROLOGUE

Three score years and ten – that's supposed to be the span of a man's life, so they say, but many in my immediate family have not been so lucky. To name but four, my only brother, my two brothers-in-law and my father-in-law all failed to make it to seventy. So my story is about my own seventy-odd years or so to date. I tell my story after being urged to do so by close friends and family, who believed, rightly or wrongly, that I have had an interesting life.

Certainly there have been several phases, each providing a variety of experiences. Phase one refers my early family background up to eighteen years old, following on to a period of national service in the Royal Air Force. The third phase is the time leading up to my marriage and the immediate years thereafter, and finally middle age through to retirement and beyond.

CHAPTER 1

FARM BOY

In retrospect I was born lucky, for two reasons: firstly because my age group just missed being involved in World War Two, but more personally because I was born into what one would describe as a middle-class land-owning farming family. However at the time of my birth my parents did not share in the family's affluence for some reason, perhaps of my father's making, so I, my sister Gwen, who was the eldest, and my older brother Roger grew up with a full understanding of what it means to be the 'poor relations' of a family.

Whether it would have been different in financial terms if my father had not been the youngest in a family of seven, insofar as he had two older brothers and they had prior control of the family's farm assets from the outset and my grandfather's largesse had somewhat diminished by the time my father was married, I cannot say. I'm afraid the vagaries of being a tenant farmer in the 1920s with a large rent to pay were too much for him to contend with, together with the fact that he and my mother contrived to produce four children in the first five years of their marriage. Whatever the reasons, within three years of getting married he was virtually bankrupt and was forced to give up his tenanted farm and find alternative work, which he did, as a farm bailiff, and we moved to a rented cottage, so I guess you could say we were living in reduced circumstances. Things then took another turn for the worse in that another sister a year or so older than me contracted meningitis, which was a very serious illness in those days, and after a short illness she passed away.

Our home at that time was in Cheshire, some thirty miles from my mother's family, and in those days at the beginning of the war that was a considerable distance for people to travel to visit relations, so in our case family support at this most difficult time was negligible. The thirties were bad times financially for farmers generally, no marketing boards or subsidies to claim, but these times were absolutely dire for my parents, who were virtually penniless with three infants to look after, and I got used to having handed-down trousers which were already well patched.

At this time my maternal grandmother (my other grandmother had died many years before) took charge, because my mother was having a nervous breakdown, and my eldest sister was taken away to live with her. I suppose I was about two at the time and I didn't see her again for five years, so quite frankly I had forgotten I had a sister. So my brother and I grew up together without much contact with the wider family. No telephones, no car, it was wartime and there was petrol rationing, so you just got on with your life.

When my sister was taken away I think it was without my father's total agreement. In the course of less than a year he had lost both his infant girls, who were little more than babies. However it was all thought to be for the greater good, as my grandmother owned a couple of farms and was reasonably well off and there were plenty of uncles and aunties around to support and spoil my sister in her early years and provide her with a good education, along with church twice on Sundays. However my sister told me in later years how much she had missed her immediate family, saying it was like being an orphan not to be with her parents and brothers until she was twelve years old. Many years later she was married, at the relatively late age of 36, but she had no children herself and I often wondered what effect her strange childhood had had on the remainder of her life. Nevertheless we remained quite close throughout our lives.

I was born in 1935, just before the war, at Knutsford in Cheshire, as my birth certificate states, on a small farm where my father was the manager. Then someone came along and bought the farm, so we had to get out quite quickly, and he got another job as a farm bailiff at Prestbury near Macclesfield, and my first memories are of that place. We still had no money but at least we had a roof over our head, albeit not for long, because for whatever reason, when I was two or three we had to move out again. My mother was going through a very bad period at this time having lost one girl less than a year old and the other taken away from her, so they were difficult times for her and my father.

As an aside, my mother's cousin Annie was an authority on the genealogy of the family and she stressed the importance of the Gerards, my great-grandmother's line. They had lived in Crewood Hall for generations until it was bought by a rich family, the Waterworths from Liverpool. One day much later, when I was in my forties, I was in the area and cheekily called at Crewood Hall. It was still occupied by the Waterworths and the man living there was a historian at Liverpool University. When I told him of my Gerard connection, he welcomed me in and proceeded to tell me about the history of the Gerards over the past 500 years. He commented that in Elizabethan times Sir Gilbert Gerard had risen to be chief law officer and Master of the Rolls to Queen Elizabeth I. Sir Gilbert died in London in 1593, having been granted estates in Staffordshire by the Queen. I visited Ashley Church, where he was finally interred in a very large alabaster tomb. While I was there the Ashley Church historian showed me the site, and said it would have taken ten days or more to transport the body to Staffordshire. When I suggested it might have been rather smelly by then, I was told it would have been put in a barrel and boiled in oil before transportation, so only bones would be in the tomb.

When Roger and I were growing up, we were repeatedly scolded by mother's aunts and told "Stand up straight and take your hands out of your pockets – don't you realise you're a Gerard?"

What a contrast to the life both had led before marriage, especially my mother, who had been professionally educated in dairy sciences at an agricultural college and had been a top-class Cheshire cheese maker in Nantwich, winning first prize at the London Dairy Show in consecutive years. She had her own staff and servants, who waited on her hand and foot. What a contrast and baptism of fire in the next five years to have four children and be forced out of house and home.

I think it worth saying that if Mrs Beckett, the wife of the cheese factor for whom my mother worked, had had her way then there would have been no marriage. She wrote independently to my grandmother to ask her to bring the budding courtship to an end, apparently saying that my family, seven of whom lived with their widowed father nearby at Pinnacle Farm, were a 'rum lot'. She was probably right, for the principal among them was William, the eldest, who at the age of 14 got a village dairy maid 'into trouble', as they called it. William was duly banished from the family by his father and put on a smallholding with his infant bride. No one spoke to them for several years. It might be difficult to understand now, but in those days the eldest son was treated as supreme amongst the siblings, all inheritance going to him, so the eldest grew up with great expectations of life, but William was quite a headstrong lad.

My father used to tell the story of how when William was first eligible to vote, he and his father set off in the pony and trap to vote in Crewe in the general election. Nothing was said about the election until they were about to make the return journey. Granddad said to William, "Well I hope you did the right thing and voted for the Liberals". William then announced that he had voted for the Conservatives. Immediately granddad said "Stop the trap, I'll not travel with a Tory!" The walk home was ten miles, so it was several hours later when Granddad was finally seen approaching in the gathering gloom, stick in hand and wearing his tall 'shiner' hat – he always dressed formally for such occasions. Needless to say, the two did not speak for weeks.

I was told by someone in my mother's family that coming as she did from relatively rich parents my mother had many suitors, but she chose to marry my father, who was a good-looking chap and a bit of a dandy.

My father had grown up in a close farming family, enjoying the pleasant things in life. There was no shortage of money, and he was the first man in the district to have a motor car. Maybe my father was mainly responsible for the family's subsequent early demise, as he was not sufficiently mature or organised at the age of 26 to get down to the hard task of family life and building his own farming business. Other uncles and aunties succeeded in these difficult times for farming, but unfortunately for us, not my parents.

So at the age of three I was on the move again and leaving Prestbury. This time my father once again got a farm manager's job in Daresbury near Warrington, but we had no idea how long we would be there. It didn't affect me as much as my brother, as he was four years older, but this gypsy existence had a profound effect on his education and social situation.

I say it didn't affect me as much because I was a little younger and able to put up with the constant changes, but I took the lesson on board in later years and resolved to make sure my children would, where possible, endure minimal changes in their schooling.

In 1938 we moved to Daresbury, the birthplace of Lewis Carroll. Our home this time was about twelve miles from my grandmother's farm, but it was wartime and we seldom saw any of the wider family. Travel was restricted by the blackout and we didn't have any spare cash to pay for tripping around. It was a period of real austerity and rationing and most people were pretty hard up, but at least we had plenty of milk, homegrown potatoes and vegetables and fruit from a small orchard.

I started school in Daresbury, and I well remember our school playground being dug up in order that air raid shelters could be built, and all of us being provided with gas masks. Most of the air raids took place at night, but I can remember as a four-year-old being sent to the school shelter when the siren went off during the day. You certainly grew up very quickly during wartime, and we had to walk the four-mile round trip to school each day whatever the weather. School transport did not exist, and very few people had cars.

Living as we did at the farm, we were made very aware of the war because the LMS (London Midland and Scottish) railway line ran just two hundred yards from our farmhouse and for half a mile or so through our pasture fields. This was the main line from Crewe to Liverpool and the north of England. And as the intensity of the war increased, the Germans came on nightly bombing raids to Merseyside. It was always the same pattern of events, perhaps a hundred bombers, the first two of which would carry flares as pathfinder aircraft for the larger bombers following, and the path followed was the railway line northward. My brother and I used to stand outside the house and watch the flares turn night into day, followed by the tell-tale drone of the bombers flying in close formation and quite low ready for their bombing mission, with a target only ten minutes away or so away. Sometimes they were heading for Runcorn or Widnes, which were very nearby, and the fires lit up the skies until dawn.

If all this wasn't enough, the army installed an anti-aircraft gun just a hundred yards from our house and this began firing at the bombers as they approached, and when they appeared on the return journey the firing started again. But this was a way of life during the blitz and it seemed to go on forever. Needless to say sleep was hard to come by, but you had to get up the next day for school as if nothing had happened.

As a side issue to this my brother and I used to trawl the fields looking for flares to see who could collect the most or find the largest piece of shrapnel. It was crucial that any shrapnel was removed from the pasture to prevent the cows from stepping on it or getting it into their guts, so we did this every morning before going to school. Then one day the Ministry of War turned up with wagons loaded with telegraph poles and proceeded to plant them all over the fields. The aim of this was to prevent the airborne German troops landing on our fields in gliders to sabotage this strategic railway line. It has to be remembered that Liverpool was the only large port on the western side of the country, and the troops and materials for the war effort coming from America were docked at Liverpool.

In 1941, it was amazing that with all these flares landing around us our hayshed was never set alight.

The Ministry had given us a stirrup pump and my father was on patrol every night together with other air raid wardens. They seemed to drink tea and smoke all night, and the anti-aircraft crews joined in as well. They were certainly exciting times and character building, and I was just five years old.

Whilst we were living at Daresbury we had a terrible experience, not connected with the war. By way of background the incident was related to the historic movement of Irish labourers coming over from Ireland to harvest the potato crops. It was a seasonal job, April to October, and thousands came over each year to work on farms all over England – it has to be remembered that until the sixties, the harvesting of potatoes was largely done by manual labour. These gangs lived quite roughly, often sleeping in makeshift quarters in hay barns or above shippons (cowsheds), and their washing facilities were pretty crude. It so happened we had four such potato pickers at our farm, and to my father these guys seemed to be good friends, but unlike him they were heavy drinkers. At about seven o'clock every night they would set off for the Ring-o-Bells pub at Daresbury to get some food and beer, and they would stagger back very drunk every night.

Anyway one night the police roused my father well after midnight enquiring if all our Irishmen were back at the farm, saying they had a search warrant to search the buildings. When they did so, one of the four was missing, so the police arrested the other three and took them away in a van. The story was related to my father by the arresting officer. There had been a drunken knife fight between our four Irishmen at closing time, witnessed by the landlord and others, and one of them had had been apparently stabbed a few steps from the Ring-o-Bells. The other three had run away, leaving their colleague badly injured, and he died almost immediately from his injuries. A very sad story, as these guys, all in their early twenties, had only a few hours before walked happily up our drive on their way to have a good night out.

One of the men, only eighteen years old, was quickly found to be the guilty one and he was hanged in Walton Prison in Liverpool soon afterwards. When not working, this young man used to play with my brother and me, and this murderous incident affected my sleeping for ages afterwards. His three colleagues remained with us – someone had to pick the potatoes! The war effort continued, and it was estimated that 10,000 Sherman tanks came through Liverpool to be loaded on trains to be quickly dispersed down to the Midlands and the south of England ready to be used much later for the D-Day landings.

Whilst I was at the Daresbury farm I involved myself at the age of six in something which virtually became a personal tragedy, and it was completely self-inflicted. At the time it was a straightforward domestic accident. One evening I was toasting bread on the open fire (there were no toasters in those days, and in any case we didn't have electricity) and I reached up from a sitting position on the floor to take the poker in order to clear the coals. In so doing I dislodged a fireside kettle full of boiling water, and this came cascading onto my legs. Almost immediately I found myself in a pool of boiling water. Both legs were very badly scalded and there were injuries to my backside also.

With the use of a neighbour's car, I was taken five miles to our doctor's surgery. At this time there had been a breakthrough in the treatment of severe scalding where large blisters were apparent on the body. The technique was for the doctor to apply some freezing agent and then with a pair of sharp surgical scissors to cut the blistered skin off, then apply some antibiotic cream, followed by a binding of the legs in my case, and then leave the injury untouched for three weeks, at which point completely new skin should have formed. Unfortunately during the three weeks I contracted the dreaded scarlet fever, and when the bandages were finally removed the wounds were found to be covered with pus and yellow matter, so I had to endure several hours of excruciating pain whilst the original dressings were removed, nearly as bad as when they cut the blisters off. Very deep sores appeared and in some places the bone was clearly visible.

I was bedridden with the fever and leg injuries for four months, and there was a critical period of a week or so when it was thought I would not recover because of the scarlet fever, but perhaps I was made of sterner stuff. Coincidentally my father and brother also caught the fever and they were duly dispatched to the isolation hospital some ten miles away, but I remained at home, being too ill to be moved. I well remember four months later, when the fever was gone, men coming from Warrington to fumigate the whole place. Remarkably, my mother remained free of the disease throughout.

My recovery was a very slow process and I was away from school for six months, mainly because I had to learn to walk again because my legs had been so badly damaged by this near-fatal illness. But I continued to have a very special regard for my mother, who cared for me virtually single-handed during this miserable period while also having to work ceaselessly to keep the farm going during my father's enforced absence in the isolation hospital. Like the rest of her family she was an avowed

Christian, and I seldom heard her complain – indeed she was always seeking to help others who she considered to be more deserving than herself. At times her disposition was almost saintly.

Although my time at Daresbury had been so packed with incidents, we were soon to move again, because the owner of the farm wanted it for a relative, so after three years we had to make a rather hurried exit. This time we went to live in rooms at my grandmother's farm. I was now approaching seven years old, and it was at this time that I met up with my sister, who by now was twelve years old and attending the grammar school at Northwich.

My brother and I attended the local council school and we had to walk a round trip of five miles each day, but this was only to last for six months because at this juncture mother's elder sister, who was married to a businessman with a thriving egg distribution business, persuaded him to take up the tenancy of a farm a few miles away in order to give us a home and a more settled existence. We were now a whole family again as my sister Gwen came to live with us, but it took a long time to get used to having her around. That was the first time in my life when I was aware of the wider family around me. Aunt Mary was the main instigator and influence in making things happen to get us going again.

Notwithstanding the deprivation caused by the war, I remember hearing of the really awful times my Uncle Frederick suffered when, like many young farmers, he was called up to fight in World War One. He was in his late teens when he went to France. Because since boyhood he had been used to handling horses on the farm, this vital experience was put to good use, for virtually all the heavy lifting was done by horses pulling supply wagons or gun carriages to the front line and trenches. Every day he saw acts of cruelty done to the animals by less sensitive comrades who would beat the poor horses even when it was obviously impossible for them to move wagons which were bogged down in deep mud.

As the fighting raged, horses badly injured by German shells were falling all the time and Fred was given a humane killer which he would use if necessary to put them out of their misery. It must have been so difficult for these young men. There were hordes of rats everywhere feeding off the bodies of these dead animals, and some used to take the chance of being shot rather than spend the night in the rat-infested trenches. Uncle Fred had a horrific war, but like many other young men returning to their farms afterwards he just had to get on with it and seldom mentioned what he had been through – no counselling for him.

Fifty years later I was involved in a sequel to this. Among the kit my uncle brought back from the war was a humane killer, which resembled a revolver. Some years after his death someone broke into the house where his widow, my Aunt Margaret, then 83, was living and stole a tool box from the garage which contained the humane killer. Some weeks later the thief was caught and owned up to stealing the tool box. The police then visited my aunt, wanting to see the gun licence and telling her it was a serious offence to own a firearm without one. The rusty old revolver was taken away and kept under lock and key at Audlem Police Station. I happened to be the executor for both of their wills, so I made an appointment with the police inspector handling the case. I explained that my aunt had never seen the pistol, which in any case was over 60 years old and so rusty that it could not be fired. It was no more than a museum piece. I am glad to say that I was successful in persuading the police to drop the charges against my aunt, and told them they could keep the gun, clean it up and raise some money for a police charity with the proceeds.

Going back to our new family life together, this time my father was an employee of my Uncle Bill, who stocked the farm with animals and bought the tractor and farm implements, so my father resumed the role of farm manager. Little did I know it at the time, but this was to be my home until I got married. However, the war was still carrying on and somehow wherever we went we managed to find a home near a railway line. This time we were very close, about fifty yards away, but fortunately it was only a branch line from Crewe to Northwich and after a time we got used to the noise of freight trains rumbling past in the night.

Occasionally troop trains carrying American soldiers would pass by and if the trains stopped for long enough, we would cheekily call out 'have you any gum chum?' Usually the soldiers would respond very generously. A great surprise one day was to see a train virtually full of black soldiers; it was the first time I had seen a black man, because in those days there were no black people living in our part of England. White troops from America did not travel with black troops – a colour bar very clearly existed in those days, even in times of war.

By this time the blitz was nearly over and apart from a V2 rocket which landed nearby, the skies were free of German planes. But on the ground it was quite different. Hundreds of tanks and guns were parked on the Northwich bypass and we used to jump on and off Sherman tanks on our way home from school. Then suddenly and quite mysteriously, within a couple of days they were gone south. We later learned that they were heading for France for the top-secret D-Day landings.

By now I was eight years old. Having been moved from pillar to post over the preceding years and in and out of four schools, together with a long period of illness, my basic education had been seriously affected, but in those days farming people did not pay much attention to educational achievement, as it was always assumed their sons would work on the land anyway. In my case events would prevent this happening, despite the fact that in my family there were relations who owned farms, perhaps as many as a dozen. So you can see my family was virtually exclusively into farming.

However this period of my life was rather more predictable, and family life was quite enjoyable. Gwen was now living with us, having spent the previous eight years living with her grandmother, and life seemed more complete; above all, father was glad to see her back. He worked very long hours on the farm, rising at half past four each morning to milk the cows, after which he had to bottle the milk and then be on his milk round at seven, and this routine was followed seven days a week. He had a great capacity for manual labour, but unfortunately he was less keen on the administrative aspects of his job. Inevitably I was expected to help on many farming tasks from an early age, both before and after the school day, but Sunday was treated as a day of rest and for going to Sunday School twice and church in the evening. Listening to radio was not permitted, no newspapers were bought other than the *Sunday Companion*, the religious paper of the day – the Sabbath was strictly maintained.

Nevertheless, at this stage in my life mine was a very happy childhood and there was no pressure from my parents to achieve intellectually. Growing up and living on a farm with all its attractions, space and amenities was, in retrospect, a privileged existence, or so many of my friends who lived in houses with small gardens front and rear seemed to think, and many of them wanted to visit and share in the farming environment, though I am not sure they would have liked the duties that went with it.

There was a downside to this. Like most farms it did not have any modern conveniences, with only part of the house having electric light, no flushing toilets and only a single cold water tap in the kitchen. All hot water had to be got by boiling kettles and I went to bed each night by candlelight. But this farm was a step forward, in so far as it was the first home to have any electricity at all. My pals only saw the glamour of farm living – I'm not sure what they would have thought of the lack of modern conveniences in their daily living. In truth the house was cold and damp and most years I had bronchitis with periods off school, and I was certainly regarded by my parents as the weak one of their brood.

1945 brought the end of the war, and a year or so afterwards I transferred from junior school to secondary school. It was no surprise to my parents that I did not join my sister at the grammar school, and nor had my brother a few years before. Maybe the upheavals and difficulties we had had to endure in early childhood had made their mark, compared to the continuity she had enjoyed. In spite of this there was no enmity between us. No one thought of failure and children generally who had attended a secondary modern did not regard themselves as second-class citizens; this was in the minds of the social reformers and politicians of the day.

In our small family of three children I suppose it was music which brought about a feeling of equality. My mother had always played the piano, so all three of us had music lessons at the age of eleven – to her it seemed as natural as breathing, and I've always thought music was the great equalising factor in our family. Gwen did least well in her attempt to conquer the mysteries of the five lines and four spaces, and I did best. When it became my turn I completed in six weeks what my tutor had thought would take six months. Within three years I had passed sixth grade at the Manchester College of Music and both my brother and I in later life went on to become reasonable church organists. In fact at the age of thirteen I was asked by the Headmaster to play hymns at morning assembly. I must have performed well enough, for I was called upon to do this duty whenever the music master was unavailable. So in my early teens, playing the piano at church and accompanying choirs and visiting soloists became a common part of my life. In those early teenage years music was a sort of conduit which allowed me to get out and about socially a few years before my parents would normally have allowed such licence.

Success in that field led to my gaining confidence and making good progress in my school work generally. Mathematics was my best subject, and I learned later that there was a logical relationship between the skill of interpreting the music score and evaluating mathematical numbers. Quick transmission of values from the brain to the fingers was the key to performance on the keyboard.

In my general education I made it to the top five out of 70 in my particular year. My mother, who really called the shots at home, made up her mind that farming was not for me – she thought I should work in a bank or have a commercial career. So at sixteen I went to college to learn bookkeeping, accountancy, basic shorthand and typewriting, and I completed parts one and two of Cost and Works Accounting, now known as Management Accounting, but I was not convinced I wanted to be a number cruncher forever as I felt I would prefer something with an operational aspect to it. I had always had a keen interest in geography and transport, so I applied for an administrative job with the railways on the freight side of the business. Having successfully completed the entrance examination I joined the freight department at Hunts Bank, Manchester. My first job was as a shipping and forwarding clerk, but I was still living at home on the farm.

My brother by now was several years into farming and the milk business, which had grown quite rapidly over the years. They ran two vans and milk distribution was by now the principal task, so much so that the animals were sold off and the milk was bought at wholesale prices at the creamery, so now to all intents and purposes the business increasingly became milk and egg retailing. The business was still owned by my Uncle Bill, and he appeared each week to monitor the business and bank the money.

So at this time in the early 1950s life had become more stable. Roger and I were able to manage the farm for a week at a time, and for the first time my parents could afford an annual holiday. Not in Blackpool; my father rather favoured the south coast, Brighton, Bournemouth or Folkestone. So he borrowed a car from a friend of his who owned a local garage. This was truly an adventure for him. On this occasion the plan was to go to Folkestone, one of his favourite resorts. He spent days planning his route – no motorways at the time, and the problem was how to get past London. But they duly set off and managed the journey. They chose a nice comfortable hotel near the promenade and all apparently went well until the next morning. My father had always been a very early riser, but he managed to restrain himself, with mother's persuasion, and stayed in bed until five o'clock. He was a fifty-a-day smoker and always had a fag first thing, so eventually he got up and stole out of the hotel at this early hour, went past a sleepy night porter and let himself out of the front entrance.

Unfortunately he didn't realise that he had tripped the burglar alarm, because he was out in the street before it started ringing. He left behind him a scene of confusion, with a hundred or so guests running downstairs and along corridors to assembly points. It was a scene of chaos, and my mother did her best to hide behind the mayhem which was going all round her. She knew who the culprit was, so she remained silent. Father meanwhile had made his way down to the promenade, hoping to get his usual morning cuppa. The only other people out and about were the rough sleepers who spent their nights in the promenade shelters, but father didn't mind their company. In fact he shared his cigarettes with them in return for drinking their tea.

Father was an adventurous man, and the next day he noticed an advertisement for day ferry trips to Boulogne. Neither he nor mother had ever been out of the country, so they decide to make the crossing, but hardly had they left port than father began to feel seasick, and this continued for the next couple of hours. However on landing he soon recovered and needed the customary cigarette and cup of strong tea. When he was given a glass of hot water and a tea bag he was not pleased. Later he commented that it was 'like cat's piss'.

Nor was he taken by French cuisine. He did not really know what he was eating, and he spent the rest of the day feeling rather hungry. But what got to him most was going to the toilet to find he had to share the entrance with women, and found himself sitting to 'do his business' next to a woman.

When they returned my father relished telling us everything about their week away. He simply said, "If that's abroad, they can keep it". There was no more to be said about the matter, and they never ventured abroad again.

Father was a garrulous chap and loved to tell his customers about his trips. He was well liked around the village for his generous ways and was seen as quite a character.

For me, National Service was now on the horizon. My brother was not called because he was considered to be a farmer and they of course were excluded, but somehow my father couldn't get it into his head that I would be called up when I reached the age of eighteen. I suppose it was because no one in the wider family had done National Service and he seemed to believe something would turn up to obviate the need, so the subject was not discussed, but as I saw my friends being drafted into one of the three services it was never far from my mind as I approached the age of eighteen. Most of my friends were placed into the army and I dreaded the thought of wearing a khaki uniform, as they looked so rough.

CHAPTER 2

NATIONAL SERVICE

———⊰✦⊱———

Just before my eighteenth birthday the dreaded letter arrived telling me to report to Liverpool for a medical and tests to determine which arm of the forces I would be expected to join. Hartford Station was on the main line to Liverpool, and whilst waiting on the platform I noticed a casual acquaintance of mine also waiting for the train. Keith worked as a bank clerk at the local Westminster Bank and to my great relief I learned that he too was going to Liverpool, and for the same reason as me. We were both little guys, about five foot six, but now together we set off quite confidently. We were both set on joining the RAF and genuinely thought we would be colleagues together for a considerable time.

Having reached the recruiting centre at Pownall Square, we filled in some admission forms. Then we had to undergo a medical test alongside a hundred or so other young men, all stripped to our waists on a cold February morning, which I recall was extremely cold. This was followed by written tests in English, Mathematics and General Knowledge, and finally an IQ test. All this took several hours, and then I was interviewed by an army officer. This was rather alarming, and I thought I had been rejected by the RAF and wondered how my friend Keith was faring, but later I was seen by a Squadron Leader. I did my best to impress him so he would accept me into the RAF, and he did comment that I had achieved a high mark in the IQ test.

I went home reasonably satisfied, although there was no sign of Keith on the train, and began to anticipate the usual wait of two or three months before actual call-up, so I was quite amazed to receive an OHMS brown envelope telling me to report to RAF Padgate in ten days' time. My friend had not received a similar letter, so unfortunately our hoped-for comradeship ended and I did not see him again for many years. I was just three weeks past the age of eighteen.

To be drafted in such quick order came as a great surprise to my family, my employer and my friends, but mostly to me. The good thing about it was that it didn't give me any time to think about it. And so on the 19th February 1953 I set off by train to Padgate via Manchester, taking with me the requested piece of brown paper and string. When I changed trains at Central Station to get on the right line for Padgate Station I noticed sundry other young men also clutching brown paper and string (we had been told not to turn up with a suitcase). I quickly realised we were on the same mission, so it seemed we should set up friendships right away as we were all in the same boat so to speak and felt apprehensive as we wondered what the next few hours would bring.

The journey to Padgate took about half an hour and I quickly realised the other guys were from all over the country. As we got out of the train I noticed several RAF trucks waiting, and as we walked onto the car park I got my first sight of the Flight Sergeant drill instructor and his henchmen corporals. They almost kicked us up into the trucks, swearing all the time, and dragged us out in a similar fashion when we drew up outside the station guard room. We must have looked a pathetic little group still in civilian clothes grasping our brown paper and string.

At once we were assembled in lines of three and marched off to the equipment hangar with a gang of NCOs bawling 'LEFT RIGHT, LEFT RIGHT!' at the tops of their voices. What a baptism of fire that first hour in the Air Force was. It was never to be forgotten. The brown paper and string were used that day to post our civilian clothes back home. With no clothes to wear, I soon realised there would be no going back.

We were then given our paybooks and told our pay for the week would be the princely sum of £1.40, but this was to be reduced to £1.10, the difference being described as a deduction for barracks damages. I cannot remember damaging anything, but things in the Air Force were quite arbitrary and I learned at an early stage never to question anything or you would be regarded as a 'smart arse', as they put it. and you would be picked on remorselessly.

In the days that followed we had some early square bashing, further tests and another medical examination, and then another interview with an officer who informed me that I had done well in my tests at Liverpool and that as a result I had been selected as POM – potential officer material. That was good news, but a couple of days later the bad news came. I was informed my medical examination had placed me in grade 4, as apparently my eyesight was not good enough, thus ensuring I would not be selected for aircrew training. At that time quite a lot of national servicemen became pilots.

Over the next few days a fair number of interviews took place attempting to get me to sign on for three years. This I declined to do, so I was abruptly removed from the POM category and dispatched the next day to Melksham in Wiltshire for eight weeks of initial training, generally referred to as square bashing. The regime at Melksham was extremely harsh for young men such as myself and discipline was absolutely rigid – there was no room for the free-spirited at Melksham.

The day started at 6 am and one was rarely in bed before 11 pm. In those early weeks I constantly found myself thinking lunchtime was tea time, because I had done so much in the first seven hours that it seemed well into the afternoon. Accordingly the days seemed endless. You were always on the move, as the day was split into many periods of activity, in and out of the classrooms, on and off the parade ground, in and out of the gymnasium, and changing uniform four or five times each day. There were always penalties of evening fatigues for the slow movers or the slow dressers, or for the guys who couldn't quite get the hang of the rifle drill.

The dreaded cookhouse fatigue had you peeling potatoes, washing plates or cleaning greasy food tins for two hours after teatime, arriving back at your billet after seven o'clock, and then you had to start your own personal fatigues around your bedspace, following which you had to press two uniforms daily. You couldn't go out on parade at seven the following morning without a razor-sharp crease in your trousers, so ironing was an everyday occurrence, and you learned to press by candlelight, as lights out was at 10 pm. You were chased from pillar to post all the long day.

National Service certainly became part of your life and the sheer brutality in mental terms had to be endured. Some dealt with it better than others, and if you had any impediments they made life difficult. I remember two chaps in particular. 'Ginger' Stubbs was in our billet from the outset of training at Melksham. His hair was very ginger and his skin was covered with freckles – the pigment was there for all to see. Unfortunately he was very smelly, and it was all-embracing. Early one day at Melksham, the corporal walked down the billet, stopped and said, "What's that bloody smell?" Ginger gave a short, plaintive reply, to which the corporal told him to get to the bath house and report sick in the morning. Ginger found his condition very difficult for him to bear, and despite using talcum powder constantly and washing his feet several times a day, he still stank. He had to sleep in some isolation at the end of the billet and his boots were place outside at night. In truth he spent as much time as he could outside in the fresh air. His was a dreadful disability, but he was shown no compassion in the RAF.

I well remember the name of the second young chap, whose story is tragic, but I will not identify him. He had an impediment which meant he could not control or co-ordinate his movements properly, and his senior officers took few steps to help him, so he became something of an outcast in our flight. When he was marching he was constantly out of step and couldn't get his arm and leg movements in kilter. He also could not get the procedure of rifle drill in the right sequence; the technique seemed to baffle this otherwise intelligent man. His body movements stuck out like a sore thumb on the parade ground and he was picked on all the time. He joined our flight of recruits on arrival at Melksham, but he told me had been there for 24 weeks or so, being constantly re-flighted because he could not master the basic skills required on the parade ground. He stayed with us until our eighth week, and then on the eve of our passing-out parade he was told he would not be joining it. That night he hanged himself in the ablution block. The demands of National Service were a nightmare that 18-year-old could not endure.

On occasion we could be utterly humiliated by events which were suddenly sprung upon us. Every morning at nine o'clock we had to stand by our beds for kit inspection. Every item, uniform, pyjamas, towels, blanket roll, wardrobe and bedspace, all had to be meticulously inspected by your flight officer, followed by his henchmen, the sergeants and corporals. If one of them didn't find fault, another did. The barrel of your gun was given special attention, although in truth it wouldn't have been fired for weeks. God help you if they found a speck of dust anywhere.

We were just relaxing and sharing a quick fag when the sergeant appeared again and bawled out, "Stand by your beds, FFI inspection!" FFI was the acronym for Free From Infection. He then added, "At the command, drop 'em! Release your braces and let your trousers fall!" The station medical officer then appeared and proceeded to walk slowly around the 20 beds, inspecting the various appendages which were now on view. The whole process was over so quickly that you didn't realise the utter humiliation you had been subjected to.

When the MO had gone the corporal told us that this would be a monthly procedure, adding "We don't any of that soft shanker around my billet." We presumed he meant venereal disease, as it was called then.

For anyone who had led a sheltered life hitherto, these episodes were a rude awakening, but we had to cope with them.

I well remember that first Sunday at Melksham. We all thought that after the past few days we would have the opportunity for a lie-in on the Sunday, so what a shock it was when at seven o'clock the Flight Sergeant suddenly came thundering through our billet, banging his baton our beds and bawling, "Get up you lazy bastards, church parade at eight o'clock!"

We immediately had to get up and put on our 'best blues', our dress uniform, and report to the mess for an early breakfast at 7.30 so that we could be ready to parade at eight o'clock. Nobody knew it beforehand, but there were a number of 'churches' in a converted hangar about half a mile away. We marched off, and when we came to this area the order was suddenly given to 'Fall out Church of England!" Probably a third of us were dismissed into one of the huts. The remainder then marched on for a minute or so until again an order was given: "Fall out Catholics!" Those who were left marched on a little further until the halt command was given again and the order came "Fall out ODs!" (other denominations). Being a Methodist I joined this queue, along with the Wesleyans, Plymouth Brethren etc, and we left two men outside in splendid isolation. The Flight Sergeant demanded what f****** denomination they belonged to, and they replied that they were spiritualists. By now the Flight Sergeant was frothing at the mouth, and he replied "We don't have any of those bloody fringe religions here, get fell out with the ODs and be quick about it!"

These were very serious interludes at the time, but on reflection they were quite humorous. There was no room for minorities or individuals when you were a National Serviceman. Good ness what would happen if we had National Service today, with people calling for human rights and so on. Let's hope there is never again any need for general conscription.

Public enemy number one was your drill instructor, better known as your DI. Certain people's names you never forget, and I have never forgotten Corporal Dalton. He was quite the nastiest individual I have ever encountered, always shouting and barking at you, suggesting that if you didn't do everything he said massive retribution would follow. He would yell at you all the time and one of his favourite threats was that he would kick you so high you'd come down with snow on your boots. I'm sure all of us raw recruits believed him, for nobody stepped out of line. One of the things I least liked about him was the way he stood ten inches from your face when giving you an order, so your face became wet with his spittle. God help you if you showed any sign of revulsion or dismay. Secretly we all agreed we would gladly swing for him if circumstances permitted it. Those eight weeks at Melksham were the longest in my relatively short life.

At least I was able get a 48-hour pass halfway through this training period. My family were all anxious to hear how I had got on in those first five weeks in the RAF and my letters to them had indicated what a tough existence it was, so they were looking forward to seeing me. I think my father thought I had been laying it on a bit thick and romancing a little, but the weekend pass seemed to be over in no time at all. Before I went back my mother had prepared me a food parcel, having heard from me that the camp food was hardly eatable but like it or not mess food had to be eaten there was no alternative. Also the rigid discipline during the eight weeks of square bashing had to be endured, and the guiding principle as far as the RAF was concerned was the need to turn a bunch of raw civilian recruits into a cohesive fighting force in the shortest possible time.

Was I glad to finally be on that passing-out parade

and away from Melksham. My next phase, for trade training, would be at RAF Credenhill, Hereford, where I was to be trained as a clerk secretarial. Little did I know that I was being put into a trade, in RAF parlance, that would lead to one of the most interesting periods of my life. On leaving Melksham my main preoccupation was the thought of going on 72-hour leave, seeing my friends at home and joyfully being free for just three days of that all-embracing disciplinary environment which was the hallmark of service life.

The city of Hereford I found to be a very pleasant place on the banks of the river Wye, but the RAF station at Credenhill was miles into the countryside, too far from the city for a casual walk there in the evening. I was soon to realise that trade training in the Air Force was no doddle. Apart from meal breaks we spent nine hours each day in the classroom being taught office practice, service administration and touch typewriting to a speed of forty words per minute, and all this to be done in thirteen weeks. Alongside this we still had parades, guard duties, daily kit inspections and many of the fatigue duties we had done at Melksham – after all, we were still recruits under training. Ultimately I gained a high pass-out mark and unlike most of the chaps on the course, who were posted to a permanent camp somewhere in the

UK or abroad, I was told I would remain at Hereford for another thirteen weeks, this time ostensibly studying speed shorthand writing and more advanced work in office administration.

So Hereford became a sort of second home to me. At weekends I regularly visited the beautiful cathedral in its picturesque setting beside the River Wye, to listen to the choir and enjoy recitals by the cathedral organist. I remember the summer of 1953 was an exceptionally good one, which leads me to another event of that year, which was the Queen's Coronation in June. The need to line the route the retinue would follow down the Mall led to constant parading and marching at all camps, because thousands of servicemen would be required in London on the day. So during May we were up at the crack of dawn doing rifle drill and marching about relentlessly. In my case it was to no avail, because it was decided that only those of five foot nine and above would travel to London to line the Mall. However, parading customary preparation (bullshit, as we called it) went to crazy levels to achieve the kind of perfection required – especially the toecaps of your boots, where the pimples of leather had to smoothed by heating the back of a spoon so that the spit and polish could be applied to the smooth toecap. It took hours and hours to get the desired effect, but everyone had to do it or the Warrant Officer at kit inspections would have our guts for garters, as he regularly pointed out.

Commanding Officers' parade was a seven o'clock Friday affair and sometimes he would keep us waiting for hours in all kinds of weather. I remember on one such occasion standing in our greatcoats with rifles. It became rather warm, and the chap next to me fainted, but I was balled out for going to his assistance and told to get back in line. Later, with experience, I learned that it was customary to 'leave him where he falls' until an officer gave the command, and if no officer had seen him it was sometimes a while before any assistance was given. Fainting on the parade ground was a common occurrence, and it was quite dangerous when standing with fixed bayonet.

At Credenhill, like most camps, airmen were accommodated in huts which housed twenty-two men with a small private room for the corporal, and in the middle of the hut was a pot-bellied stove with a coke bunker beside it. It was a devil of a job to get it lit, but in the cold weather it was vital or you virtually froze to death – no carpets on your bedspace, which was about two square yards, just brown linoleum which had to be polished every night, after which we had to walk on strips of blanket attached to your boots to save marking the gloss finish on the linoleum. The floor was inspected every morning after breakfast and I remember one corporal who took a delight in throwing a bucketful of coke down the billet and then walking on the coke and grinding it into the linoleum before telling us 'The floor is a mess, get it polished'. But there could be no retaliation – we just questioned his parentage.

Notwithstanding, life went on at Credenhill and I became rather good at shorthand, getting the desired rate of 130 words per minute. At passout I was given a Certificate of Merit for being the best recruit on our course, and it was duly presented to me by the Commanding Officer, who later said that if I signed on for a further year I would be given further training as a court shorthand writer and be given the immediate rank of sergeant and a job at the Ministry in London, and from there I would be sent anywhere in the world wherever a Court Martial was being held. I considered the offer, but on entering the service on day one I had never thought of serving more than two years. I thought many times afterwards what a wonderful experience it would have been, and a sergeant at eighteen was unheard of.

My final duty at Hereford in December 1953 was to go to the assembly room to be told of my posting after training. We sat there wondering what the future would hold. Most of my friends got home postings, which meant somewhere in the United Kingdom, while some were sent to the Far East, which meant Hong Kong or Singapore, and others were posted to the Middle East, which was Egypt, Iraq or Aden. This was considered to be the worst place because of the intense heat, but three of us were posted to Second Tactical Air Force, which meant Europe, or more precisely Germany. We all got three weeks' embarkation leave and were then to report to RAF Lytham near Blackpool, which dealt with all personnel going abroad. Once again I had to break away from a group of friends I had got to know rather well, but that was the way it was in service life.

When I arrived home toting my kit bag over my shoulder and told my parents what was next in store for me, my mother commented that when I had entered the Air Force she had never thought I would be sent abroad as it only seemed a few years after the end of the war with Germany. All agreed it would be better to go there than Egypt or Aden, which were such unhealthy places. Anyway, I was to have Christmas at home, and at least it gave me three weeks in civilian clothes, I didn't care much to go about in uniform whilst at home.

I fondly remember that that Christmas my mother

spoiled me a little, knowing that afterwards she would not see me for a considerable time. As for girlfriends, I didn't have a particular one, or going away for a long time might have been more difficult.

And so to Lytham. The accommodation there was appalling – old Nissen huts with no form of heating, and this in the middle of winter. We slept in our greatcoats over our pyjamas and the food was atrocious. Thank goodness my mother had given me a food parcel before leaving home. The only good thing about my stay in Lytham was that we spent New Year's Eve in Blackpool. We rolled home in the early hours having had a good night out, and it turned out to be our last night in England, for early in the morning we were put on a troop train en route to Harwich, via Accrington of all places, as I noticed peering through the grubby carriage window. It took seven hours following a very circuitous route and we arrived in the afternoon to be immediately put on a flat-bottomed troop ship called the *Vienna*.

It was an awful trip across the North Sea to the Hook of Holland. There were 1500 soldiers and airmen on the ship and the overnight voyage was to take ten hours, supposedly arriving in Holland at six in the morning. The accommodation was frightful. Three decks were fitted out with racks of wire mattresses three high with scarcely any walking area between the rows of racks and no storage space for kit bags. What was more, we all had to remain below deck to consume our iron rations and water, and that was where we stayed for, quite soon from the ship's movement we knew we were under way. This flat-bottomed ship was soon wallowing about, and before long people were being sick all over the place and our kit and equipment was covered with the wretched stuff. I was pleased to have a top bunk, because those below suffered the most in this dreadful state of affairs and you slept with your boots on to stop someone being sick in them and prayed for morning throughout a sleepless night.

I can tell you we were delighted the following morning to hear we had reached the Dutch shore. We had spent the night in semi-darkness, no portholes, just the rumbling of the ship's engines. I've been across the Bay of Biscay many times since but I have never seen the sea sickness to match that on the *Vienna*. We were glad to stumble up three flights of stairs out of this prison-like ship into some welcome fresh air and be put on a troop train heading for our destination, RAF Bückeburg, a transit camp about twenty miles from Hanover.

I was intrigued by the journey. Having left the docks we skirted around a devastated Rotterdam and headed into the flat Dutch countryside and its bulb fields. I noted the dykes and the people riding their cycles on them and soon realised why it is called one of the low countries, because the landscape was completely flat, so different from the hills and valleys I was so used to in England. There were very few cars and everyone seemed to cycle in this ideal environment for it.

We journeyed through Holland to the German border, where the train was attached to a massive German steam locomotive which was better able to cope with the more undulating terrain we would see later on in the day. The train travelled through the Rhine valley to the German industrial heartland. Although the war had finished nearly seven years before, the following two hours travelling through places like Dortmund and Essen still revealed scenes of the utter devastation caused by the American and British air forces. As we passed by the Krupp steelworks the whole area for mile after mile was flattened, with hardly a house standing and very little sign of life. I was told later the people were living in holes in the ground, like cellars.

Yes we had the blitz in London and other cities in the UK, but the scenes unfolding before us as we travelled on through Germany were a horse of a different colour. The British people could never have imagined it in their wildest dreams, and it must have been horrific to endure.

Late in the evening we reached Bückeburg, having had just iron rations (dry biscuits and water) through the day. It was over 36 hours since we had had any proper food, so we were quickly taken to the station mess room for a meal. Here, for the first time in my Air Force existence, we had delicious food. There was scrambled egg, grilled bacon, and those lovely German sausages, cooked beautifully by German cooks, and what was more, tea without bromide. What a feast compared with what we had to put up with in England, where sometimes the lumps of porridge or custard were as big as golf balls and bacon was served raw. So if nothing else, it seemed we might get some reasonable food in Germany, and that proved to be the case – no need any more for food parcels from home. But then the cooking was supervised by the GSO, the German Service Organisation, civilians who worked for the RAF in many service roles.

The following day we were segregated into groups for transfer to our ultimate destination. I was to be sent to Headquarters 83 group at Wahn, about 10 miles from Cologne. Once again on the train journey we travelled through badly-damaged towns and cities, and Cologne itself, a city the size of Manchester, was like one huge bomb site. Several road bridges across the Rhine were being restored and some temporary pontoon bridges were still in use, but the railway bridge across the river seemed apparently untouched because only a stone's throw away was the famous steepled cathedral in all its glory. Here we left the train and were packed into a waiting bus to be transported the ten miles to RAF Wahn, the former Luftwaffe airfield which was to be my home for the next six weeks.

Mentioning RAF Wahn, I recall that one day while we were there Sir Winston Churchill was flown in by Transport Command for a meeting with Dr Adenauer, then Chancellor of West Germany and the driving force behind its remarkable recovery after the war. The meeting was to be held in Bonn, a few miles away. All the dignitaries received a formal welcome, and I was part of the welcoming guard of honour for Sir Winston. Transport Command was the arm of the RAF responsible for moving vast quantities of cargo, engine parts and so on around the world, and it was well known among RAF bods that unscrupulous types used it to spirit away masses of war surplus goods back to England. These scallywags among our ranks formed associations with contacts in the UK, and in the 1950s millions were made through supposed 'war surplus'. It was rumoured that as 'Winnie' got off the plane several compressors were pushed onto it for the return journey to the UK. Mobile compressors were a favoured item and there were always plenty of them hanging around, as their main use was for starting jet engines. They had arrived from the USA in their thousands during the war and they were now surplus to requirements.

People of my age will remember the constant adverts in the national press for 'war surplus' goods. Some smart servicemen made a lot of money out of them, some quite legitimate, but there were many scallywags around and RAF and USAF aircraft were used to shift cargoes from place to place without proper controls.

Strangely enough life was much more comfortable in Germany. We lived in a modern centrally-heated barrack block with proper washrooms and bathrooms, parading was kept to a minimum and there was plenty of time to indulge in sporting activities, both indoors and out. My clerical duties commenced, and I was allocated to the personnel department in Group Headquarters dealing with manning requirements at the eight operational airbases which formed the group, but most of the extensive training I had had at Hereford was under-utilised. I spent most of the day filing papers and making amendments to manuals, and it was all rather boring. Our living accommodation was adjacent to the operational station and the role of the squadrons was mainly night flying, doing photo-reconnaissance over the east and west borders, so the downside was that we rarely got a good night's sleep because of these night fighters taking off all night long seven days a week.

Another downside was the extreme cold, especially when we were on guard duty on the windswept open airfield. In an attempt to keep warm we would wear our pyjamas under our tunics topped with our greatcoats, but a four-hour stretch was really too much to bear – I'd never realised what a cold country Germany was.

The German nationals, not surprisingly, were very hostile towards RAF personnel generally, so we were advised to have our civilian clothes sent out from England before we ventured out into the city of Cologne at weekends. It was understandable when you saw first-hand the way people were living. Incidentally, I believe Cologne was the first city to be chosen for a thousand-bomber raid. In renovation the main streets were the first to be rebuilt and the shop windows were illuminated with brightly-lit shop signs, but if you ventured just a few yards down the side streets the houses were still flattened and the people were living literally in holes in the ground.

Rather surprisingly, the houses in the best condition were those in the red light area, quite an extensive area of perhaps a square mile or so. Such was the state of poverty in post-war Germany that females from sixteen to sixty strolled the streets trying to make a mark, and at the time there were twelve marks to the pound sterling. Prostitution was a big way of life for women trying to feed their families, who were living in dire poverty. Women seemed to do all the work, as 20 per cent of their men did not survive the war. It had become known that RAF people had a free allocation of two hundred cigarettes each week and these girls would give anything for twenty fags – what a world it was. Needless to say this whole red light district was designated as an international out of bounds area and anyone found there by the RAF police, who of course patrolled the area, was in deep trouble.

Despite all this there was evidence of bright lights in the city, things were getting better and food was available. Restaurants were open and so were the night clubs. Our own Ken Colyer was the resident trad band in a cellar night club in Düsseldorf, and we used to go there quite often. In fact it was rather a paradox, because back in England in 1953 shop sign lighting and some street lighting was not allowed and food rationing was the order of the day. Some of my more sceptical friends posed the question, 'I wonder who won the bloody war'.

After a few weeks I was moved, together with a couple of linguists, to the headquarters of 2nd Tactical

Air Force, which was the controlling unit for all air operations in Germany. The three of us had to travel by ordinary train the 300 miles from Cologne to Hanover. This was the first time I had felt uncomfortable amongst the German people. Some got out of the carriage when they saw RAF uniforms and spat on the floor as they left, and such was the tension I was glad when we arrived at Hanover. While I was there I remember a royal visit from the lovely Princess Margaret, and we were all lined up for her inspection. She was in her early twenties at the time and we all agreed that she was a beauty. This was at the time when she was having an affair with Group Captain Townsend, so the visit appeared to have an ulterior motive.

The headquarters were located at a place called Bad Eilsen, quite near to Hanover and not far from the East/West border in a quite palatial set of buildings. I understand this former royal palace had been requisitioned from some noble family soon after the war. In happier times Bad Eilsen had been a spa town and country holiday resort, and it was certainly in an upmarket area with large houses a mile or so away. Little did I know at the time that I was embarking on the most interesting and exciting part of my national service.

The day after arriving at Bad Eilsen I was told why

I had been kicking my heels at 83 Group Headquarters. They explained that I would join the Intelligence Secretariat as secretary to the Chief Intelligence Officer, 2nd Tactical Air force. During the previous two months the Air Ministry people in London had been having me positively vetted in order that in the future I could handle top secret and other highly classified documents. The CIO who I was going to work for was a former Battle of Britain bomber pilot who was highly decorated and had been a prisoner of war in Colditz Castle, the notorious German POW camp.

Back in England a few weeks earlier, my father had been surprised to be visited and questioned as he was doing the milking over a prolonged period by two Special Branch police officers from London. These two officers also spoke to other people in my local area who had known me as a teenager, eliciting information about my particular interests, my political leanings if any and whether I was active in a trades union or left-wing socialist organisations. No mention was made of why this information was required, and my parents finally wrote to me asking if I was in some kind of trouble out in Germany, but by this time I knew what it was all about. So now I knew what I was going to be doing for the foreseeable future. It has to be remembered that when you were allowed to see secret information, you had to remain silent for 30 years or face 14 years in jail, so it was not until relatively recently that I was able to divulge to friends and relations what I did during my RAF service.

Through lack of practice I had difficulty keeping up with dictation speeds when my boss was preparing intelligence appreciations to be sent to the Air Ministry in London, all highly classified. The Intelligence Secretariat contained about thirty officers and men and the boss had two wing commanders as his deputies and numerous squadron leaders as section heads. One in particular I was going to meet many years later in different circumstances. Squadron Leader Bird had the responsibility for security in this particular intelligence cell and he was aware that Eastern Bloc spies and sources would always be trying to break through the security of our department, through physically breaking into our offices to make available information which might be useful to foreign agents of the Soviets. So from time to time doors would be sealed with cotton during the evening and the following morning, they would be closely examined to see if the cotton had been broken. It was all rather cloak and dagger stuff. One of my tasks each night was to clear all waste paper from offices including carbon paper and incinerate the lot before any GSO cleaners were allowed into the offices.

Everyone was seen as a potential Russian spy, and we knew they were all over West Germany, for after the 'hot' war ceased in 1945 the cold war with the Soviet Union started virtually the next day.

One remarkable security incident stood out in my memory. We had a large room and upon one wall a detailed map of Eastern Europe indicated the locations of all bases and airfields in East Germany, Poland etc. This map was constantly updated as known movements of opposing forces took place. In the evenings roller shutter doors were pulled down to cover the wall and locked in place, but of course during the day the roller shutters were in the up position. One day a GSO window cleaner was thought to be lingering in his job, so immediately he was brought down the ladder and sure enough he had in his possession a micro camera stuck on the end of his brush. Whilst cleaning he had also been taking photographs of our wall charts – yes, he was a German spying for the Russians. Immediately all the window panes were painted inside and it was my job to do it, as we didn't trust any contractor in the department after that break in security.

One has to remember that in the fifties the Soviet Bloc had an overwhelming advantage in conventional forces of tanks and manpower over us and the Americans. The rest of Western Europe was virtually powerless and the

French were changing their government every year. The two issues that kept us from a third world war were our shared intelligence over possible Soviet action and our tactical nuclear battlefield weapons. The Soviets did not have these at this time, and Stalin was mindful of what happened to the Japs, so it was a positive restraint on the Red Army with their millions of men under arms. It was our department's job to constantly monitor aircraft to prevent a surprise attack being launched westwards by the Russians to turn the cold war back into a hot one. Long before GCHQ existed at Cheltenham we had a string of listening stations along the Iron Curtain gaining information for us. The English have always been good at intelligence gathering. Our department combined with MI6, and our sources, who were generally foreigners, operated on the ground as spies, not forgetting our military attachés and men working abroad in our embassies in places like Warsaw. All these activities combined together to give us intelligence information, but it all started with some foreign national (the source) lying on his belly on the perimeter of some Polish airfield taking photographs of their aircraft.

One should be aware of the background and context of all this, namely that just a few years before over 20 million displaced people were milling about this area of central

Europe, most of them homeless victims of the war, and it was difficult to know their nationalities, whether they were Polish, Dutch, Ukrainian, French or Russian, and millions were still around in 1953 trying to escape to the West from the East because the Soviets were treating them so badly. It fell mostly to the Americans and the English commissions to resettle and bring some order to this sorry state of affairs and provide these people with a future. At the same time it was easy for the Russians to infiltrate their agents into our organisation. But there was a need to have some system of liaison between the occupying forces of Berlin, so a local arrangement was agreed. BRIXMIS (British Commander in Chief Mission to the Soviets) was an organisation set up by our intelligence which was very much into counter-intelligence and espionage in Eastern Germany. It was countered by a similar organisation called SOXMIS (Soviet Commander in Chief Mission to the British). Both organisations had the freedom to have agents move about each other's territories around Berlin and there were about forty people in each mission. It was broadly speaking a gentlemen's agreement to allow an element of spying on each other's territory and sectors of Berlin. This was cat and mouse stuff, but it was a way whereby agents were able to get into others' areas of command. I remember BRIXMIS agents had a fleet

of VW Beetles and Opel Kapitans at their command,
with spare registration plates available in the hope that a
change of registration would throw their pursuers in East
Germany off their trail, but BRIXMIS agents were very
good at getting information about what was going on in
East Germany and their information was vital for us.

Aerial photography was another source of information
which regularly came into our intelligence section. Even
fifty years ago high-flying aircraft could take pictures
which gave very precise information, and you could read
markings on planes parked in airfields deep behind the
Iron Curtain. Regular flights took place to RAF Gatow
down the air corridor to Berlin under the guise of flying
food and materials. The level of intrigue used was quite
incredible; it included dummy cases to disguise them from
the Russians, who had spies on the ground at both ends of
the corridor to mislead them as to what we were loading
on to the aircraft. In fact they were carrying cameras and
were operated by RAF people throughout these trips. The
first cameras were only capable of carrying out vertical
photography. When the Americans had perfected the
technique of oblique photography we flew planes much
higher and the scope for aerial intelligence gathering was
much greater, but we knew that East Germans probably
knew what we were up to so our aircraft had to keep

strictly within our air corridor during these flights, and the cameras were treated as cargo and only fitted when the plane was airborne.

But back to my daily round and common task. The classification of documents I typed for the boss was very important and at the end of the period of dictation he would always say what stamp was to be used, either SECRET, TOP SECRET or possibly COSMIC, the classification above TOP SECRET. I well remember one day that a delegation of MPs and civil servants from London came to our department and there was a frantic few minutes to clear all papers away and lock down all wall charts, because most of the visitors had not been positively vetted and of course had to be viewed as security risks, no matter how titled they were. The Americans were extremely hot on security and we had an American USAF officer as a liaison man keeping an eye on us, but our contact with the French, Dutch and the Belgians was very much on a need to know basis. In fact the UK/ US EYES ONLY classification was strictly adhered to. But one has to remember that at the time the UK trades unions and Labour Party were riddled with communist sympathisers who thought that the Russian Revolution and what followed was great for the people of Europe. This view was certainly not held by the Americans.

As I said earlier, it was a time when we and the Americans shared information on the development of battlefield nuclear weapons, which we needed to counteract the undoubted superiority in numbers held by the Warsaw Pact countries. The Americans were very nervous about leaks in other nations' intelligence services and the French were the least trusted of all, and quite rightly so, because a Frenchman had been complicit in the Russians getting the atomic bomb. The Yanks never quite forgot their quick departure from the war in 1940. Some still referred to them as 'cheese-eating surrender monkeys', not to be trusted. And some of that enmity still prevails today.

Being involved in such exciting and interesting work seemed to make my national service life go by very quickly, but others who were stuck in very rudimentary jobs found their time in the Air Force pretty boring, so I had to count myself extremely lucky to have such rewarding and interesting tasks to do. However it wasn't all work. For short-stay national servicemen like me we had leave centre. Whilst at a place called Winterburg in the Harz mountains I had my first opportunity to do some skiing, and a little later, when our HQ moved down to Mönchengladbach, more sporting activities were available to us. Mönchengladbach was the site where the headquarters staff of the Army, Navy and Air Force were to be integrated in the NATO command structure of Northern Forces Central Europe, so this new camp became a massive project, self-supporting with its own infrastructure of roads, hospital, swimming pools, houses as married quarters and barrack blocks, and of course a massive HQ building.

What impressed me most was the enterprise by the Germans had shown in just a few months. I recall walking past a construction site where married quarters houses were going up, and the next day the house was built and finished. Yes, it took them just 24 hours to build a semi-detached house. The German building industry was brilliantly organised. To start with, the work went on day and night whatever the weather. They covered the whole house structure with a tent, so adverse weather conditions did not interrupt their work. Nearly all joinery products for doors, windows and roofs were pre-manufactured to exact sizes and heaters were used to dry the cement and plaster, while the interior painting was left to the tenants. The planning was strictly followed, and you could say the whole house was engineered, not built. When they finished it was their custom to put a flag on the chimney, and I was amazed as I walked past each day on my way to the office when another house appeared with a flag on top. It was by using these tactics and work methods that the post-war German miracle was made to happen, and I could see quite clearly that the once mighty German economy would soon be back to full steam ahead.

Rather sadly at this time in England there were constant strikes in key industries and who-does-what disputes in ship building, particularly on Tyneside, inspired by politically-motivated trades unions. Conversely there were eager ship workers up in Hamburg and Bremen just waiting to take the work away from the English, and they did. It was surprising how soon Hamburg rose from the ashes until it was the largest shipbuilding city in Europe. I often thought it was a shame that having been on the winning side, with nearly all our factories and industry intact, we didn't take advantage of the situation while two of our principal competitors, the Japanese and the Germans, were smashed to the ground.

However, back to the RAF. My two years were coming to an end in February 1955 and I well recall having a final interview with Squadron Leader Clifford, who had responsibility for personnel in the Intelligence Section. Previously we had had several chats about service in the Air Force and he tried to persuade me to sign on for a few more years with a commission in mind, or some sort of extra service, but I think he knew I would not be induced to spend more time at Her Majesty's pleasure. Perhaps I had given him the impression that I thought national service got in the way of a young man's career, and to some extent he was right. However, on the leaving form which every airman has to have on termination of service so that it can be given to a prospective employer, I noticed that although my sickness, attendance and conduct record was stated as exemplary, the final remarks section at the foot of the form bore the sentence 'this airman does not take kindly to service discipline'. I took great exception to the use of these words and pointed out that I had never been on a charge form during the whole of my two years, but despite my protestations, he was not prepared to alter the wording. It was a good thing I had a job to go back to, but his remarks left a nasty taste in my mouth, so to speak. When I travelled to England the following day, and eventually to RAF Innsworth near Gloucester for my demobilisation, I left without any regrets. Only some time later did I realise just how much I missed the comradeship engendered by the way of life in the Royal Air Force.

On the night I arrived home from Gloucester, rather strangely, there was no welcoming home party – all the household had gone to bed, so it was not exactly the homecoming I had anticipated. It was getting towards 11 pm when my mother came downstairs to let me into the house. She said they had expected me earlier and when it got to ten o' clock they had all gone to bed. And that was my homecoming from the RAF.

Strangely enough I nearly did have to do further service in the RAF, for in 1956 I got my call-up papers again and was told I had been transferred to class 'H' of the RAF Reserve. It was at this time that the Egyptians and their leader, Colonel Nasser, unilaterally nationalised the Suez Canal, which in fact was owned by the French and the British and was regarded as an international waterway. The French and the British then occupied the canal zone, which quickly led to a war with the Egyptians, so I and many others waited to be called back to the RAF. It didn't last for more than a couple of months, because the Americans did not back us and we were forced to withdraw. The then Prime Minister, Anthony Eden, was forced out of office and the French took a dislike to the Americans which has lasted for seventy years. In the same year, 1956, the Russians savagely put down an uprising by the Hungarians when several hundred people were killed while the Americans turned a blind eye. So much for the 'special relationship'.

CHAPTER 3

BACK TO
CIVVY STREET

When I returned to civilian life I was just two weeks over the age of twenty. I immediately returned to my position as a shipping clerk in the goods department of British Railways at Northwich, later travelling to Warrington, just a few miles away. I think some people at the time thought it a little odd that a farmer's son should be working for British Railways, but in truth I had always had a fascination for railways, having lived alongside them from a very early age; I had watched the streamlined blue carriages of the Royal Scot passing at speed through our fields every night on its way to Glasgow, and knew every night that when the milk train went by at seven o'clock it was my bedtime. In a sense I grew up with railways and the associated link to transport and traffic movements, so I was something of a logistics freak from the start!

Life at home carried on as before, my brother working on the farm, but by this time my sister had completed her studies at college and was a qualified schoolteacher. I found civilian life rather humdrum and missed the company of colleagues and the comradeship that went with it, so returning to civilian life was quite a shock to my system and it took several months to settle down. I played a fair amount of football, and following on from my table tennis success in the RAF, I played two or three nights each week in the Mid Cheshire League. I got involved again in church life and taught myself to play the church organ, and before long was appointed as a church organist; Friday night was youth club night and I took up the friendships I previously had, and when an elderly gentleman resigned I was in charge at weekly choir practices.

There were plenty of nice girls around, but at this stage none had taken my fancy, so there was nobody special for me, unlike several of my friends who were 'going steady', as they described it or even married.

Eventually I got used to home life again. I suppose farming was in my blood, so as an interest I started keeping hens and the eggs produced were sold on the milk round. This went on for a couple of years and I suppose I built up a stock of two hundred or so birds, but then one fateful night a fox got into the hen cote and killed over a hundred. When I went to feed them that morning the place was a horrific scene with blood and feathers all around, and those that were not dead were cowed in the corners of the hen cote. I was told afterwards that a fox will kill until it is physically exhausted and becomes caught up in the frenzy and hiatus of its own killing appetite but will leave with just one of the hens it has killed. Those people who have sympathy for the fox should see at first hand the awful devastation to livestock that a single fox can do – it kills randomly, not simply to feed itself as most animals do, and ever since that day I have been a strong believer in fox hunting as a means of controlling their population growth.

Following on from my part-time poultry farming I started to keep pigs, about twenty at a time, and I bought them as six-week-old piglets after they had been weaned from the sow. They were termed 'store pigs' and the idea was to feed them until they were sufficiently developed to become bacon pigs, which usually took about six months. I fed them before cycling off to work in the morning and at night I fed them again and mucked them out, and at this time I managed to merge my clerical duties with my livestock rearing without too much difficulty. In addition I sold eggs and dressed poultry to my colleagues in the office. I suppose I was a bit of a wheeler dealer.

Then in the summer of 1956 my father bought an old car, a 1938 Singer saloon, 15 horsepower and a four-seater. Until then the only vehicles we had were vans for delivering the milk and they were not to be used for social purposes. On the arrival of the Singer I quickly got around to having some driving lessons from my father, and at the second attempt I passed my driving test. This opened up a whole new world to me, although the car had to be shared by the four of us.

Something even more significant happened at that time, when a certain young lady joined the church choir. Pat was dark-haired and tall for 15, and to me and I'm sure to other people she was a very good-looking girl. At first I thought the five years or so age difference was too great – she was still at the local grammar school. But I must say I was greatly attracted to her and she, being quite a forward young lady, returned my affections – she became my first real girlfriend.

So started a very private romance, but I knew from the start it was love at first sight. The church was, I suppose, the catalyst to our developing romance, for the youth club and choir activities, together with church on Sunday, gave us plenty of opportunities to see each other, but this was only at weekends and she lived on the other side of town about five miles away. Because of the age difference we wanted it to be a secretive affair and did not want others to know, especially her parents, who if they had known about it would surely have attempted to bring it to an end. Pat was only allowed out on Friday and Sunday nights on the premise that she was meeting her grammar school friends at church activities, so when I walked her home on these evenings I quickly got on a bus when we got anywhere near her home, and this kind of clandestine approach to our 'forbidden' romance seemed to add excitement. However, when she left school approaching the age of seventeen and went to work at the Westminster Bank, I finally met her parents. She was anxious that this should happen to put the thing on a proper footing, but I felt her father still thought I was too old for her.

Having got myself a girlfriend of some distinction, I started to realise I would have to take stock of my working life and to carve out a career in order to eventually be able to 'keep her in a style to which she had become accustomed' if subsequently I was going to marry her, and that was something I definitely wanted to do in a few years' time, so all this became a tremendous motivator for me.

So opportunities had to be sought. Work study was a management technique that many companies were getting involved in and I'd heard the British Transport Commission, our parent company, was thinking in these terms. I noticed that the National Council of Labour Colleges, a government-inspired agency, was doing introductory correspondence courses on the subject.

I completed a six-month course working mainly at weekends, and then a month later, quite amazingly, six jobs as Time Study Operatives, as they were called, appeared on our circulated vacancy list. They were seeking people with some knowledge of the subject, though professional training in industrial engineering would follow, although the jobs were located in London. They say you have to be in the right place at the right time and also that you make your own luck, and so it happened, because I had done that course on work study, that I knew more about the management technique than most other applicants. Accordingly I was offered one of the positions in London, and my days as a shipping clerk were over, and from that day forward, virtually all my career was based in London.

The general idea when I joined the Productivity Department at HQ in Euston Road, London was that after twelve weeks engaged on the methods of producing bonus schemes for goods department personnel, I would work on schemes at any location between London and Carlisle. Each project might last up to six months and I would be away from home Monday to Friday each week. As you can well understand, this promotion made a fundamental change to my working life and also to my courting arrangements, but it was subsequently to lead to accelerated promotion through the job classification for salaried staff because the technical aspects of these jobs were evaluated highly in the organisation. In fact in the next six years I achieved higher grading than most people did over a career spanning forty years and got myself a first-class pass for use throughout the system before I was 30 years old.

In these early days when I was based in London but going about the country basically doing rate fixing, I was aware that further study would have to be undertaken in Work Study Practices, and sure enough the company was sending guys to the British Iron and Steel Federation Staff College at Leamington Spa for two-year courses in Industrial Engineering. This was a sandwich course with periods of study at the college interspersed with periods out in the field. There were about twenty students on each course. The working time at the college was 8 am to 8 pm with two breaks of thirty minutes for lunch and tea with dinner late in the evening, and on Friday we travelled home to be back for 8 am on Monday. From day one we all felt the tremendous pressure, especially because every Friday afternoon we had to take an examination covering what had been taught in the previous days, and on returning the following Monday, if your mark was not good enough, you were de-selected from the training course as being considered unfit for further training. So each Monday morning some people were sent home, and as the course went on our numbers dwindled. People were just put into taxis and sent to Leamington Spa railway station; it was very cruel. So we spent some of the weekend swotting and preparing for Monday. I think it was the second period at college which really sorted the men from the boys.

I recall one of our lecturers, a doctor of mathematics seconded from Warwick University and quite an unpleasant individual, stepping up to the blackboard, chalk in his hand, and with a great flourish writing a very involved formula and saying, 'Gentlemen, on Monday I'm going to introduce you to the mysteries of statistical method and this formula is to do with the law of probability, so can you please swot up on your algebra at the weekend'. Needless to say this man ruined everyone's weekend, and worse, he went on to do the same for the next twelve.

I recall very clearly that first Friday homecoming and telling Pat with some trepidation what lay ahead, saying to her that she had been at grammar school more recently than me, so she might be able to help me with this move into higher mathematics. She replied that her knowledge of such things was pretty useless. I suggested that she was a bank clerk and good at figures, but she said bank clerks were good at arithmetic and nothing else. She then related a funny story to emphasise her point. One day her former maths teacher had come into the National Westminster Bank branch where she worked for some cash. He was rather dismayed to see her there and commented that if Pat Johnson (her maiden name) was looking after her money he should perhaps transfer his account to Barclays.

I wonder what today's university students, doing perhaps 15 hours a week study, would have thought of our study period, which was nearly 60 hours a week. At Leamington Spa in 12 weeks they brought you to the standard achieved at university in one year – it was indeed cramming. Fortunately I had studied Maths to 'O' level in the RAF. There were only ten survivors in the end, but we were then allowed to join the Institute of Industrial Engineers as fully qualified Work Study Practitioners.

So now I had a professional qualification, but the pressure had been intense for a 25-year-old. This training stood me in good stead when I eventually went into industrial management, but I often said afterwards that I wouldn't have inflicted those final weeks at Leamington on my worst enemy.

Although I was qualified, I now had to get down to using the techniques of method study and work measurement out in the field. I continued on projects, and most were located in the large industrial cities of Liverpool and Manchester, thus giving me more time at home, but more importantly time with Pat. At weekends we often travelled by car into Manchester for concerts at the Free Trade Hall to big bands such as Count Basie, Stan Kenton and Louis Armstrong, in fact anywhere big band stars were appearing, but we could only go to such places when it was my turn to have the car. On one such occasion we went to Sale Locarno. Humphrey Lyttleton was doing a one-night stand and we both liked trad band music. All went well until on the way back to Northwich at about midnight the gear stick snapped off and we were stranded in the middle of the Chester Road without any means of traction. It was an old, decrepit car and I was used to holding the driver's window up with a clothes peg and carrying a stick on the back seat to dip the petrol tank. Few of the instruments worked anyway, but having no gear shift in the middle of the night twenty miles from home was a real problem.

I noticed that there was about two inches of gear lever sticking out from the transmission tunnel, which gave me an idea. The two of us pushed the car into motion and then jumped aboard. I rammed the car into gear by kicking the stub end and we proceed home in second gear, gauging the speed of the car very carefully in order to get through the many sets of traffic lights. It took us a long time to get home, but once we were out of the urban area it was much better.

The next problem was how to drop Pat off. Finally I stopped on a hill near her home for her to get out, then rolled the car down the hill, banging it into gear to get me home some three miles away.

The following morning I had some explaining to do to my father when he found the detached gear stick on the back seat. The tractor had to be used to tow the car to the local blacksmith, who was a friend of my father's, and he welded the gear stick back into position. I would point out that gear sticks in those days were about two feet long and were prone to snapping off, and this car was well over twenty years old and had done a high mileage.

Fortunately, the family was lifting its horizons on the car front and the four of us each put in £100 to purchase another car. It was a giant step forward when we bought a three-year-old Humber Hawk, with a column gear change – column changes were popular in those days because they allowed a bench seat in the front, giving seating for six people, and what a marvellous courting car it turned out to be. Ah, the memories!

Now that we had our new wheels the Singer had to go, so it was spruced up for sale. When cleaning under the rear seat we found a massive gaping hole where the body had corroded very badly and the road was clearly visible below. As a matter of interest I'd always found the car very uncomfortable when travelling in the rear, and now I realised why. My brother and I fixed it by firstly fabricating with steel struts the rusted and corroded area, then covering this with a piece of tarpaulin sheet, then putting in a large hessian sack stuffed with hay to add volume and comfort before putting the back seat in position. The rear seat had never been so comfortable, although it was something of a fire hazard. Funnily enough it was bought by a local policeman for fifty pounds, and I can remember seeing it around the village for years – I often wondered if he ever looked under the rear seat, but I suspect not.

Now we had a full six-seater, and we often went with two other couples to dances at weekends when it was my turn to have the car. These were great times. However, like many young men, I'd always hankered after having a sports car, and knowing that marriage was beckoning, I thought it was now or never. So without really consulting anyone I indulged myself and bought a red Austin Healey Sprite convertible sports car for £500, which was most of my savings. I suppose my parents thought it would have been better used as a deposit for a house, but they never interfered with my personal life or sought to give advice. Although at the age of 24 I was still living at home I was working away most of the time and had successfully carved out a career for myself not remotely connected with farming, so in terms of my career and future prospects they were not in a position to tell me the way I should go. In truth I'd been ploughing my own furrow and job career wise since the age of sixteen, so my £500 indulgence didn't seem to me to be such a big deal. Anyway, I was earning good money and thought I would be able to save for a house deposit very quickly.

Pat and I enjoyed our sports car rides to Blackpool, Southport and the North Wales holiday resorts and down to Bournemouth for the week. In those glorious days of carefree motoring in 1959 and 1960 there were very few cars on the road, very few parking restrictions, no yellow lines and no roadside speed cameras to think about, and if you had an open-topped car as we did, you never feared it would be stolen or the contents removed. People driving around today cannot imagine the pleasure driving gave you in those halcyon days, and we never regretted the expenditure which gave us those years in an open-topped sports car. I suppose you could view it as a phase of our life before marriage. Although Pat was only 19 she was keen to get married, but it was not at the forefront of my mind although we had become engaged during the year, but I was very aware how attractive she was to other men and if I hesitated too long I felt she would soon be snapped up by someone else. So together we set the date in April 1961 to get married.

After the wedding we moved into a two-bedroomed bungalow in a small village in mid-Cheshire, for which I paid £2000. I had managed to save £500 for the deposit and I took out a mortgage for the remainder. I remember on the day the deal was struck with the estate agents my father came along with me and insisted on making out a cheque for £200 for the 10 per cent deposit. I thought, that's okay, he's giving me some money towards it, and I knew by now he could well afford it because around that time both mother and he had received several inheritances, so their financial position was completely different from just a couple of years before, but no, after a few weeks he asked for his money back. Since my father and mother had now become reasonably affluent they had persuaded my Uncle William to sell them the farm, because up to that time both my father and my brother worked for him. I think he was a little reluctant because my father had never successfully run a business although he was a very hard-working chap, so with my mother's persuasion the farm was transferred to my brother Roger, who was a much better manager of money. By this time he was in his early thirties and wanted to consolidate his future. So for the first time in many years my family at the farm had become self-supporting.

Talking about Roger, I must add a few words about my relationship with him. Although we had grown up together in a small family, our careers were now poles apart. I had a profession was and was largely employed in London, while he was now ostensibly a self-employed milkman, employing my father. He was a talented musician, and served as a church organist for many years. Since his youth he had been a keen sportsman; his enduring love was cricket, and he played at club level for nearly 40 years. However, he had a preoccupation with making money, and his goal was to be a millionaire, which he achieved, by constant hard work and shrewd investment. At the age of 50 or so he was able to indulge himself in cricket. He joined a group of Manchester businessmen who yearly went on cricket tours to cricketing countries like the West Indies, Australia, South Africa and Southern Rhodesia (now Zimbabwe). Later he would recall opening the batting at Newlands, Cape Town, and spoke very warmly of the splendour of Salisbury (now Harare) and the warmth of the Caribbean.

Having been largely estranged from him years, I saw more of him after he retired and sold in his business when he was fifties, and when I was in the North, I would call to see him on my way back to the Midlands. On one occasion I visited him after attending a board meeting in Manchester, and we were having a drink and a chat about old times. In the course of the conversation he said to me, "Of course you were the one with brains in the family, not Gwen or me". He told me that being a milkman, as he had been for most of his life, was the most boring occupation you could imagine, but it did not stop him making money.

Rather a tragically, a year or so later Roger developed a brain stem tumour, and he died before he was 60. I remember visiting him in two Merseyside hospitals. His last few months were desperately unpleasant and painful. Life is not fair. It is odd to think that I could live perhaps 30 years longer than he did, but that's the stark reality of life.

Returning to my career, it was around this time that Dr Beeching, my ultimate boss, was brought in by the Conservative Ministry of Transport, Ernest Marples, who had run a large civil engineering business, to be in charge of British Railways. He was recruited to bring in some business knowledge into this failing public service organisation and to deal with the massively overmanned operation, together with duplication of line services within all regions of British Railways, which were a relic of pre-First World War railway development. British Railways virtually ignored the fact that the internal combustion engine had been invented 40 years ago and road transport had emerged for the movement of people and freight, and it promised to be a much more flexible mode of transport. Evolution had moved from the canals to the railways and now to the roads, and people wanted to have choices to drive and own their own transport. BR employed nearly 600,000 people and yearly made a loss which the public purse could not afford, at today's prices amounting to many billions. The same could be said of other nationalised industries created just after the war, like steel and coal mining.

The Beeching organisation sent teams of industrial

engineers and economists to all regions of the UK, and at this time I was promoted to the status of Team Leader and sent to Barrow-in-Furness to head up a team working in the North West up to the Scottish Border. My patch extended all the way up the coast to Carlisle and all branch lines, private sidings and quarries inland from the large towns of Workington and Whitehaven. Bear in mind that at this time there were coal mines, steelworks and chemical factories, so it was quite a busy little area, but it was beginning to decline, although unfortunately manning levels still reflected those required in better times. One would find signal operators, crossing keepers, shunters and the like still about, although their work had ceased some time ago; there were shunting engines around and no wagons to shunt. The railways were something of a sacred cow in this post-war Great Britain, and there was duplication of services all over the country. For example, you could get from Manchester to London by four different routes, and premises and labour costs were far beyond what was coming in from fare-paying passengers, so rationalisation had to take place, and under Beeching it did.

For my part in the North West, one branch line which linked Cockermouth via Keswick to Penrith was losing an absolute fortune. A three-carriage train was being used on this route throughout the day and an analysis of ticket revenue and travelling passengers showed that on many trains during the day only a handful of passengers were travelling. Historically the Cockermouth, Keswick and Penrith railway had come into existence in the last century before road transport came into being, and of course the railways had been a much better way of travelling from the west coast to Penrith than using a stagecoach. Also farmers used this new railway to get their livestock to market at Penrith instead of using drovers. But those days were over, and we had to close this branch line. Bus services were introduced to give an appropriate service at a mere fraction of the railway cost.

I recall that one of the greatest headaches was what to do about the massive losses that were being incurred on suburban commuter services running into London and large cities like Manchester and Liverpool, because commuter travel was increasing rapidly and unfortunately for the train provider the more people travelled during the peak times the greater the loss, because the plant and equipment needed to satisfy the travelling public was only being used about fifteen per cent of the day and lying idle in sidings for the remainder. Massive losses were incurred, and commuters were considered to be public enemy number one to the train operators. In those days there were no subsidies, so the government was made aware that railway finances would have to be reviewed. There were at the time, and still are, complaints from commuters that fares were too high, but commuters had to understand that all those extra carriages were bought for their use and for nobody else.

Just before moving up to Barrow I had a rather strange experience early one morning when travelling by road into Manchester to work, a distance of twenty miles or so from my home. I set off at 5 am in order to meet up with someone at 6 am in Manchester. There was hardly any traffic around as I joined the Chester Road, and I only noticed one Transit-type van going in my direction, so I quickly overtook him. Suddenly a large Rover came behind me going quite quickly, overtook me and slowed down almost immediately in front of me, forcing me to brake. By this time we were only doing some 15 miles an hour and he was veering about the road, so at the first opportunity I passed him, only for him to repeat the process, so we were back to travelling at 15 miles an hour until we had to stop at a set of traffic lights. I was being badly delayed, so I went past him again. By this time we were leaving the country area and were approaching Altrincham, but we were back down to a very low speed and if I tried to overtake him he would move over to the centre to prevent me although it was early morning and quite dark. At the next set of traffic lights I drew alongside him and because we were now in a 30 mph area I thought he would behave himself, but no, he came racing past again. Then he misjudged a corner, hit a street light and crashed into the front door of a police station. I carried on for about a hundred yards and was just in time to see him staggering across the road towards a policeman who was walking towards him.

A moment or two later the van driver who I'd seen about half an hour before came along. He stopped and said he was glad to see me join the road at Northwich because this crashed driver had been bothering him all the way from Chester. I was in a hurry and he wanted to get to Manchester Fruit Market, so we continued our journeys. Obviously the man had been as drunk as a lord and the police would take him into custody.

I usually bought the *Manchester Evening News*, and I was quite amazed to see an article at the foot of the page which told of a doctor making an early morning visit to a sick patient on the outskirts of Altrincham being run off the road by the driver of a red sports car just outside the police station, and saying the police were seeking anyone who had seen the incident. Needless to say I ignored the whole thing. What a scallywag this doctor must have been

– perhaps he was high on drink or drugs. And what of the police? I kept the van driver's registration number just in case I needed a witness, but I never did – sometimes life is stranger than fiction.

On the domestic front things had not gone so well. After we had been married for about two years Pat had become pregnant and we were looking forward to our first child. This of course was before pregnant mothers had scans to determine the condition of the expected baby, so she went through the full term of the pregnancy. It wasn't until the actual birth took place that we were informed that the baby's head was malformed, and our little girl died soon afterwards. I remember very well the process I had to go through registering the birth and then immediately seeing the undertaker who had to deal with the burial of our baby girl. We were both terribly upset, and Pat had to endure the experience of seeing all the other girls in the maternity ward going home with their babies. We got over it after a while and she returned to her position as a cashier at the Westminster Bank.

We carried on with our weekend social life, and one particular Saturday we had a chance meeting with an up-and-coming pop star. It was our habit to travel to a restaurant to have dinner and call at a nearby country club for an early drink, and as I approached the bar I saw this rather dishevelled guy wearing a long camel-coloured jacket with long shoulder-length hair tied with a pink bow, a really scruffy guy. He was on his own having a drink and just propping the bar up. There were only another three or four people in the bar and he was minding his own business. As I was buying the drinks alongside this man, I recognised him as the singer Tom Jones. We nodded to each other and I asked him what he was doing in our regular watering hole. It transpired that he was doing a one-night stand at the local civic hall. He would have been no more than about twenty years old at the time. Within a couple of years he had some big hits which transformed him in to an international performer. What was even more striking was the way he changed his appearance – long hair gone and smart suits – and he had become a singing sex symbol and idol all over the world. He appeared to be a big man on the stage, and when I told people he was below average height they didn't quite believe it.

My thoughts careerwise were now focusing on the wider issues of transport, logistics and distribution and I felt my future should be in road transport with the demise of freight transport in the rail industry. Also, now that I was married I thought that after seven years or so on the road living out of a suitcase, I should like a more settled existence. I saw and applied for a job in Hemel Hempsted entitled 'Assistant Traffic Manager'. This would of course mean a move away from mid-Cheshire.

Of course we still wanted a child, and before long Pat was pregnant again. We were delighted when our doctor informed us that she would be having twins. We thought to ourselves that this would make up for the earlier loss. The one downside was that although we still lived in Cheshire I had taken up my new job in Hemel Hempsted, so I was away Monday to Friday. We had some very good neighbours and I knew they would keep an eye on her whilst I was away during the week, but we decided to sell our bungalow so that I could look for another house in the south, so for this interim period Pat moved in with her parents, who lived just a few miles away.

As she neared the end of her pregnancy, because she had become so big with the twins, It was decided that she should be taken into the maternity unit at Nantwich for a few days of examination. When I returned to Cheshire that weekend I of course visited her, but on this particular Friday night after visiting hours I was called into the office by the duty doctor, who told me they suspected one of the twins was again malformed in the head and it was likely to be a hydrocephalic. This baby girl would not survive long after birth, and the other twin might not survive either, because of the difficulties of such a multiple birth.

I was absolutely devastated by this news, which had not been imparted to Pat, and of course that had to remain so. I visited twice on Saturday and Sunday knowing that within a few days she was going to hear some dreadful news. I also kept the news from her parents. On the Monday morning I travelled back south to avoid suspicion and to convey to her that everything was okay, as you might say, with a heavy heart knowing full well that the next few days were going to be very grim for Pat.

Late on the Monday afternoon I had a call from the maternity hospital telling me that for a few hours they had been attempting to induce the births and something would happen later that night, so I got into my car and drove the four hours back to Nantwich. On arriving I was seen by Dr Smeeth, the consultant, who had been present at the birth and was given the good news that the boy, born first, had been fully examined and found to be in perfect health, but the baby girl was not expected to live much longer. I then went to see our baby boy, who was lying on Pat's chest. She was looking quite radiant in spite of what had gone on over the past fifteen hours.

A few days later she came home, this time with a baby, and what a glorious homecoming that was. A few days later I had to go through the tedious process of registering the little girl's birth, followed by seeing the same undertaker to see to the burial. Some time later we saw a specialist. He advised us not to have any more children because if it was a girl the chances were that it would be imperfect again, so we had to be satisfied having just the one child. I have often reflected that people who have multiple children without difficulty don't know how lucky they are, or maybe how unlucky we were.

Three weeks after the birth of Paul, Pat moved down to Hemel Hempsted. She had never seen the house before because she had been so heavily pregnant at the time, but she had trusted me to purchase one that would suit us both, and when she walked in with baby in arms I was very pleased to show her our new three-bedroomed detached home, complete with a cot in the front bedroom. The move had really worked like clockwork.

CHAPTER 4

RETURN TO THE NORTH

———✦———

A nd so began some of the happiest years of our life together, cherishing those times with our new baby. Pat was surely born to be a mother. I used to go home at lunchtime to see them; we never went out at weekends, nor did we think of having a babysitter, as he was too precious to be left with anyone and both sets of parents were now 200 miles away. Pat very quickly made friends with one particular person she met when visiting the post-natal clinic. That was Jean, and she and her husband Bob became great friends. The friendship lasted for many years after we had left Hemel Hempsted, but sadly at a relatively early age Jean died of cancer, leaving Bob and her two children behind.

Returning to life at my new employer, the reason I had been chosen was because they liked my industrial engineering background, and immediately before taking up my functional duties as Assistant Traffic Manager I was asked to look into their present system from production control into warehousing and their distribution and transport system, which for the whole of the UK was handled from Hemel Hempsted. The company had grown rapidly over the past ten years and we had a steel rolling mill for the production of steel for the materials handling business. That was our principal activity, but we also produced nuts and bolts in large quantities, and we had a section making household goods, so the senior management thought maybe some changes should be made, so who better than their own kind of in-house consultant to investigate and report on their present activities and make recommendations for the future? I was guided by their own operations research department.

Ultimately I got into the role I was recruited for and had a small staff. I was supposed to advise on the use of our vehicles and manpower with the aim of getting better utilization, and of course lifting productivity, but working in the manufacturing side in a very enterprising company was all new to me. Nonetheless I was enjoying my work

in private industry following years in a nationalised organisation. The principal difference was the speed and ease of decision making and one had the freedom to act with great flexibility, the
exact opposite of the bureaucracy I had been used to.

The company honed my personnel skills with courses on recruitment and staff assessment and appraisal, and the company employed a rather enlightened approach to the personnel function. A Cambridge professor who had a background in industrial psychology advised on planning the personnel policy. Another thing virtually unheard of at the time was that first names were used throughout, so Norman, the managing director, talked on similar first-name terms to the tea lady, Edith. Likewise all used the same dining room and the same toilets. It was completely different from the world I had been used to, but it worked very well.

However my stay in the south was coming to an end, because following further studies by our Operations Research Department it was decided to have a regional depot for warehousing, distribution and sub-assembly work and this depot would be located at Leigh in Lancashire. Furthermore I was to be promoted and moved to Leigh to set up this new organisation. I recall the MD saying to me, 'You recommended the new system, now go and manage it'. Soon after this l had a company car to go with the job. So single-handedly I planned the size of the warehouse we would need and set up the vehicle fleet which was to cover the area of operations from the Potteries to the North of Scotland, doing several trips to survey the area north of the border and recruiting a dozen or so staff, administrative, stock handlers and vehicle drivers to do the job.

It was while I was at Leigh that I met what I would call my first real 'scallywag', who happened to be a heavy goods vehicle driver. Drivers are a mixed bunch of individuals; some are of a quiet disposition, others noisy and self-opinionated. Some are highly intelligent men who had chosen not to listen to their teachers whilst at school and who, through a lack of formal qualification, had just drifted into driving as a job of work, one which is relatively well paid compared to other occupations. But one thing they all had in common – they liked their freedom and their ability to pass their day without close control. As 'kings of the road' it was a different challenge every day, meeting different people. Not for them the paralysing control of a factory with a supervisor breathing down your neck, or the repetitive boredom of having to work continuously at the speed of a production line. No, drivers want a job where the individual's initiative and innovation allow a level of personal achievement, fighting to get the job done, despite belligerent customers, bad weather and roads congested with ever more and more cars – their public enemy number one. Cutting corners is a favourite objective, because that can lead to a little bit of freedom or rest during the working day – it certainly is not undertaken with the objective of returning to the depot early. The only reward for getting back early would be the management increasing the workload on that particular journey. No, their prime objective was to make time to get their heads down for the odd half hour, or perhaps do a 'foreigner' for a friend or relation. Having control of a wagon gave drivers a useful asset which they could easily use to earn a few extra pounds and the goodwill of their friends.

Years ago when drivers just filled in a daily journey log sheet, they were open to wide interpretation and abuse if the individual had the guile and ability to deliberately falsify a particular day's work, and many supervisors would be unable to spot a faulty log sheet. I remember on one occasion a driver was using his vehicle for some private furniture removals in Manchester when he was supposed to be travelling between Halifax and Huddersfield. These cowboy drivers had great difficulty in coping with the introduction of tachographs because of the discipline they brought.

Yes, I had my fair share of cowboys and scallywags in those early days of the seventies, when I was in my late twenties and cutting my teeth as a depot manager in Lancashire. I was looking after a workforce of perhaps twenty people, including some eight drivers, doing multiple deliveries with a fleet of eight-tonners. It was mostly day work, but twice each week we had to do nights away travelling up to Scotland, a round trip of approximately 750 miles. The drivers took turns covering our Scottish trips and it was a condition of employment that all would participate.

On this occasion it was a driver called Len, who had to make ten drops across a broad belt of Scotland, Glasgow to Edinburgh with the most northern town being Stirling, a distance of well over 700 miles. Clearly a night away would be necessary, so he was to head up on Tuesday morning with a six o'clock start from the depot and his vehicle would be already loaded for him the previous night.

On this particular Tuesday I was late leaving the office, about seven in the evening, and as I was driving down the East Lancs Road I saw just in front of me a company vehicle. I was baffled as to who this should be, so I caught up with the lorry and to my amazement it was

Len, who should have been 300 miles away in Edinburgh. So I went home and rang the depot to enquire whether he had arrived back at the depot. 'No' was the answer, 'he's having a night away in Edinburgh'. I replied that I had seen his vehicle here in Lancashire just thirty minutes before, to which the foreman said, 'Well there's a rugby league match at Wigan tonight and we know Len is a Wigan fan.'

It was a mystery, and I spent most of the evening thinking about it. I got to the depot early on Wednesday, wondering whether I would see Len, but there was no sign of him. In fact he did not appear until 4.30, the usual time for the end of a two-day trip. I had given my secretary prior instruction that I wanted to see him in my private office, and eventually he came into the general office and I asked him if he had had a good trip and enquired if the digs had been OK in Edinburgh, to which he replied that they had. I then offered to pay his subsistence allowance for the night away. He was about to sign the chitty when I asked him if he really wanted this money and suggested he should think carefully before accepting the cash. I then suggested that he had not spent a night in Edinburgh, and told him I had seen his vehicle on the Wigan road the previous night.

He quickly became very red-faced and uncomfortable,

for he knew the game was up. Subsequently I gave him a written warning for gross misconduct, but I was very interested to know how on earth he had travelled over 750 miles and successfully completed his ten calls in one day. At the outset he admitted that the rugby match was his great motivation, and he then also admitted that instead of starting at six o'clock he had started at three o'clock and had been in Paisley before seven. I said I still could not see how he could do the remaining five calls in the time, which included drops in Stirling. He then had to admit that he had a Scottish friend, also a driver. From time to time they helped each other, and on this occasion this man had done the Stirling deliveries in his own wagon, thus reducing Len's travelling time by two hours. Needless to say his log sheet for this journey was a work of fiction and his speedy driving must have been a hazard to public safety. Nevertheless, the resourceful Len had completed his workload and enjoyed his Tuesday night rugby league match. Yes, he was a man of great innovation, and if I had not been late in the office the previous night, nobody would have been the wiser. What a scallywag.

With men like Len around, life was never short of incidents. A little afterwards I had an early call when at home from the transport supervisor to tell me that Len had not tuned in and that an urgent delivery for Hull was part of his day's work. We had a construction team on site, so we had to get a relief driver immediately to get the job done. Anyway, nothing was seen of Len until I was told by my secretary at around ten o'clock that he was on site and wanted to see me urgently. She went on to explain that he had three of his children with him, all below school age – it was well known he had quite a brood. So I suggested she look after the children whilst I talked to Len.

I asked him what had happened, making it clear that he should have been in his lorry on the way to Hull. Then followed a remarkable story which at the outset I was very reluctant to believe, but which subsequently turned out to be completely true. At two o'clock the previous night he had left his bed to 'take a leak'. He had not slept very well and said his wife had been snoring and grunting, which was apparently quite normal for her. When he got back into bed his feet came in contact with what he thought was a hot water bottle, but in the darkness he heard a plaintive cry. On investigating, he found to his great astonishment a new-born baby at the foot of the bed. His wife was still snoring and fast asleep. I really didn't know whether to laugh or cry for him.

He then said that after this discovery he had quickly

arranged for an ambulance to take wife and baby to the maternity hospital and apparently, the latest news was that both wife and baby were doing fine. It was quite incredible. I asked, 'Didn't you or your wife have any idea that she might be pregnant?' To which he replied, 'She's a big woman and she has them without any difficulties'. The only aside was that a couple of nights before she had some indigestion which he referred to as 'a bit of bellyache'.

When he began his story I thought maybe it was some sort of fabrication, but in the fullness of time it turned out to be absolutely true. It was the talk of the depot for some time, and when I mentioned the episode to my wife she was lost for words.

Where his love life was concerned, Len did put himself about. A few months later I happened to be at a company sales conference at a large hotel in Blackpool. In the course of events I had a meeting and a drink with a regional sales manager who disclosed to me as part of our conversation that he had seen one of my goods vehicles parked in a side street overnight close to where he lived. I thanked him for this information, but I knew it should not have been there, so the following morning I asked my transport manager why he had allowed one of our vehicles to park overnight within twenty miles of the depot. He came back with the reply that all vehicles on that date had returned to the depot – the only vehicle absent was Len's, and he had been in Scotland. So we quickly concluded that Len was up to his old tricks again. When I confronted him he admitted that he had done another runner, on this occasion to visit a big blonde in Blackpool! So I am afraid this time Len had to go. But what a character! Being a driver gave him the freedom his lifestyle required.

A few years earlier I had encountered Brian, another scallywag. He was quite a bright chap but very unpredictable. Sometimes he was a very good worker, but at other times he complained that too much work and effort was expected from him, and he made our journey planners' lives a nightmare. I came across Brian when I was managing a fleet of vehicles at a location 20 miles north of London, with an area of operation from Southern England up to the Potteries. Again it was multiple-drop deliveries, and Brian drove a five-tonner. One day he was given a route commencing at Watford then travelling north up to the M1 to Coventry, Birmingham, Wolverhampton and north as far as the Potteries, then driving south to Worcester and Swindon and back to base. That was about twenty calls and roughly 480 miles, so it was considered a two-day trip with a night away at

Stoke on Trent, then travelling back the following day.

One of Brian's main interests in life was football, and on this particular day, England happened to be playing Germany at Wembley with an eight o'clock kick-off. My manager, like me, was keen to go to this match, so off we went. As we were travelling just south of Watford we picked out a vehicle in the darkness, obviously going to the match. It was Brian's.

When he was interviewed the following morning to ascertain how he had completed his two-day workload in a single day, he admitted that he had started at five o'clock and missed two deliveries because they were not open, but the remainder seemed to be legitimate. He said he had taken the statutory rest periods, but I was very sceptical about this, and we knew he had been driving well above the speed limit. It was quite a remarkable day's work, but we didn't want that kind of thing. Once again, if a scallywag driver is motivated enough, by football in this case, he will pull out all the stops if it suits his purpose.

I had a quite different experience whilst at this depot, rather a sordid affair which led to a group of employees going to Pentonville Prison, including one of my drivers. He had got caught up with other depot workers stealing stock from the warehouse over a prolonged period. Three people were involved in this scam: a forklift truck driver (to load the vehicles), a security man at the gatehouse (to wave through the lorries) and of course my driver. They were a clever gang, never stealing too much, so the losses of stock were not highlighted, but the pilfering went on for a year or so and stock worth several hundred thousand pounds was stolen. The organiser of this affair was, quite remarkably, the company Safety Officer, who spent part of his day in the main gatehouse and was able to manipulate the devious operation.

I will leave the subject of scallywags for a moment and return to my career and my new position in Leigh. After nearly three years away in the south, I did suggest that we could perhaps live in Cheshire again. Maybe it would mean travelling twenty miles or so to work daily, but that would not be a problem. Anyway Cheshire was a nicer place to live than South Lancashire, so we would be near to both sets of parents and could renew our relationships with former friends in the area, but we always look back with great fondness at those years of living just outside London when we had our new-born baby to ourselves.

So we returned to mid-Cheshire and purchased a large detached bungalow on a corner plot with plenty of land around it, and it certainly provided us with a lot of work to get the garden in order, but my father was always a willing hand.

From time to time I joined up with friends to go to a football match in Liverpool, Manchester or indeed Stoke. On one such occasion my brother, my cousin and a mutual friend packed into my father's ageing Hillman Minx and set off to Manchester to see United play Liverpool at Old Trafford. Because of the rivalry between the two sides it turned out to be a good match, and we all thoroughly enjoyed it. However a strange incident happened on the return journey. My brother, who was driving, was always something of a speed merchant and quite enjoyed a competitive if somewhat reckless style of driving when there was plenty of traffic around, and there was plenty around on this occasion heading away from Manchester on the main road through Stretford and Sale on the way through Altrincham and home to Northwich. On this part of the road there seemed to be countless sets of traffic lights before one got onto the open road. My brother as usual was driving close to the car in front when the lights were green in order to get through before the lights turned to red – he was certainly an 'amber gambler'.

We were closely following an old VW Beetle with a large rear bumper and equally large overriders fitted, and as we approached the next set of lights the Beetle suddenly braked. We were only a few feet behind. The brakes on the Hillman were not good and you usually had to pump the pedal in an emergency. The combination of this and poor shock absorbers managed to arrange things so that when we came to rest our front number plate had lodged on the rear bumper of the Beetle, pressing its rear end down and sending the front shooting in the air. The front was suspended about two feet off the ground, and immediately we saw the very angry driver trying to get out of his car. We all burst out laughing as it was such a comical scene, but the other driver was not at all amused. We inspected the damage to find it was negligible, so my brother gave him twenty pounds to calm the guy down and pay for his trouble.

Two things were in our favour. Firstly there were no police around, and secondly there were plenty of spectators in other cars, so with the help of a dozen volunteers we soon lifted the Hillman off the back end of the VW. In the end the driver had a good laugh about it with us. It really was a crazy incident.

It was nice to be back home living in the bosom of the family. Paul was my parents' first grandchild and my mother tried to spoil him. Pat would have none of it, but my sister, who by now had many years' experience teaching entrance age children at primary school, was very impressed with him as a three-year-old. He was starting to read at a very early age, so she encouraged Pat to spend time reading with him. We had known he was bright a year earlier when he had a fascination with the Dinky cars we bought him, and one day when he was sitting in the rear of our car he started shouting out 'Viva!' 'Escort!' 'Cortina!' etc as cars went by. Of course, to him these cars were full-size replicas of Dinkies. My sister thought his powers of recognition and coordination were remarkable for a two-year-old. With her advice he became an early reader and was reading so well before the age of four that when he started school he had a reading age of seven. Pat had been around in those early years to help and encourage him in his development, but it seemed he didn't need any pushing. He would ask question after question and soaked up knowledge like a sponge.

A few years later I was told by the company to expect another move, this time to Gainsborough in Lincolnshire. The company had taken over a firm which made building products, and they wanted to move my operation into this factory. In addition they had run out of space at the factory in Hemel Hempstead and were planning to move all nut and bolt forming machines into Gainsborough and install a steel rolling mill. I was to be factory manager in charge of all operations. I was really excited by the prospect, which included the promise of a directorship in two years' time, but of course it meant moving again.

I started the new job in the spring of 1970, and again it meant living out of a suitcase from Monday to Friday. I sorely missed Pat and Paul, wo was not yet of school age. I had to get up very early each Monday morning to make the three-hour car journey over the Pennines, sometimes through deep snow, to Gainsborough, and as the weeks went by staying at the White Hart four nights a week.

A strange thing happened one morning when I was having breakfast at the White Hart. I spied in the corner of the dining room a figure from the past, Squadron Leader Clifford, the man who fifteen years before had signed my leaving form when I was returning from my RAF service in Germany. It was rather a shock to see him sitting there in civilian clothes. I was filled with curiosity, and when he rose to leave I went over to him and introduced myself. He of course remembered me, for we had been in RAF Intelligence together for some time, although he had been a senior officer and I was just a lowly national serviceman. We chatted for a while, and it emerged that since leaving the service some ten years before he had worked as a company representative, and this area was his patch. We left it at that and I went to the office as usual, but later that morning my secretary asked if I had time to see a rep, and who should be shown into my office but Squadron Leader Clifford. What a change in roles. I was now the senior person and he was a representative seeking my business.

Over the next few weeks Pat came over with me on a couple of occasions when we were looking for a property, but she declared quite soon that she was not looking forward to the move to Lincolnshire. She didn't like the area and the schooling was not as good as in other places, and I had to admit it was quite a run-down area and she had got used to having her family around her.

I let a few weeks go by and then one morning while I was still at Gainsborough I noticed a job advertisement in the *Daily Telegraph* for a distribution manager with the Distillers Company in Liverpool, so I applied immediately for the position. DCL, as it was better known, was the largest drinks company in the UK, having in its portfolio whisky brands like Johnnie Walker, Dewars, Haig and White Horse, as well as the largest gin company, Gordons, and many other big brands like Pimms. Indeed it was the bluest of blue chip companies, and for an aspiring distribution man food and drink was the place to be. The vacancy had arisen because DCL had made the decision to set up an in-house distribution company as a subsidiary encompassing all brands which had formerly looked after their own distribution, and Liverpool was the region chosen for a pilot scheme.

About four weeks later I got an interview at their headquarters at 21 St James Square in London, quite a palatial building and formerly the home of the Bowes-Lyons, the Queen Mother's family. Because of my circumstances they agreed it could be held on a Friday. I was seen by the Company Secretary and a Personnel Manager and I thought it was a reasonably good interview from my point of view, but I was told there had been a lot of interest shown, so I didn't raise my hopes too much. Two weeks later I was called in for a second interview, and this time I sat in front of a panel of four people, including the Managing Director, who was strangely silent and let the others do most of the talking. I thought I had done pretty well, but obviously not well enough, because the following week I received a letter of rejection.

I continued my travels to Gainsborough and then several weeks later, out of the blue, I received a letter from DCL offering me a similar position but located in the West Midlands, a place of 'pleasant amenity', as the MD described it. They knew I would have to give three months' notice to my present employers, and said they would negotiate an earlier release. Pat and I visited the site over the weekend, and this time Pat was agreeable to the move, so I accepted the offer.

The salary and fringe benefits offered by this quality employer were most attractive. Of course it meant a third move in five years, but Pat and I thought that if we were going to move again it would be better to do it before Paul started at primary school. He had been attending a play group as a four-year-old. I certainly did not want him to experience constant disruption, as had been my lot in my crucial early years.

So in 1970, aged 34, I was off to the West Midlands, still living out of a suitcase from Monday to Friday. We started selling our home in Cheshire and seeking a fresh one in the Midlands, but this time I was determined to seek a location not far from my place of work. This wasn't easy, as were gazumped twice before finally buying a house in Kingswinford. In the interim period I was living comfortably in the Himley House Hotel, which at least gave me the opportunity to focus fully on my new job. As a matter of interest the hotel was the former hunting lodge of Himley Hall, owned by the Earl of Dudley, a great friend of the Duke of Windsor, who in the 1990s was said to be the richest man in England. It was well known that he was having an affair with the beautiful Lady Dudley. Specifically I was to monitor progress with the building of a new bonded warehouse and distribution centre, recruit some 50 people to staff the various functions and then conduct training courses to bring everyone up to standard before 'D Day'.

The culture at DCL was that managers were self-motivating general managers with a high degree of autonomy to act across functions, so there were virtually no Head Office staff other than an accounting function. The only thing that was really new to me was the Customs & Excise requirements within a bonded warehousing system. I was given a few manuals to read, but thankfully I had recruited a bright admin manager who very quickly developed the skills needed to ensure duty paying and stock records were up to Excise standards. I just signed the duty cheques. I well remember a particularly busy day just before Christmas when I signed a cheque for over a million pounds – that was a lot of money in the seventies.

Security was another aspect of my business which became all-engrossing, but then whisky and other spirits were high-value commodities. I remember it used to take nearly half an hour to alarm and lock the warehouse every night, but again I had an excellent warehouse manager and I never had to put myself in the position of being a keyholder. Don had been a bonded warehouse manager in Liverpool in an earlier employment, and I had travelled up to Liverpool to recruit him and persuade him to relocate to the West Midlands.

Don was a very interesting character, having been a career Merchant Navy officer, graduating from Liverpool Nautical College as a teenager and going to sea as a trainee ship's officer just before the Second World War. Before college he attended Wallasey Grammar School and one of his fellow students was Harold Wilson, the future Prime Minister. Don was at sea throughout the war, and for another fifteen years, and he had a host of stories to tell of life at sea during the war years. He was mainly engaged on Atlantic crossings with convoys which were nightly threatened by German U-boats. One night in 1943 his luck ran out and his ship was torpedoed 400 miles off the West African coast. The ship was bringing arms and supplies from America for the war effort, and suddenly around midnight in a calm and quiet sea there was a terrific blast. It was apparent to the 50 or so crew that they had been torpedoed, and the ship began to sink very quickly. The Captain and Don, as First Officer, gave immediate orders to release the two lifeboats, abandon ship and get into them, and all the crew, including those below deck, were saved. Don was in one lifeboat and the Captain in the other. They rowed frantically away from the sinking ship, and as they were doing so the U-boat surfaced suddenly about two hundred yards away. The skipper, speaking perfect English, addressed them from the conning tower through a loudhailer and gave them navigational references, telling them to row due east to the African coast and wishing them good luck. The U-boat then quickly submerged, leaving the men in absolute silence on the moonlit sea. Five days later, despite having only a compass and the stars for navigation, they reached the African shore.

Naval chaps always have a great many stories to tell. One day after the war Don made a trip to South America and part of the cargo was a prize Hereford bull to be used in that country for breeding purposes. Unfortunately it was a very rough crossing and the bull became very seasick. When they eventually reached port they were welcomed by the local mayor and the corporation all decked out in white uniforms and a brass band playing. As the bull was lifted up by the ship's crane, the wind got up and it started rotating. It suddenly let out a roar and opened its bowels on the assembled gathering, turning their uniforms an unpleasant shade of brown. The band played on.

Don was some fifteen years older than me and I learned a lot from the way he managed his subordinates. I never saw him lift a case of spirits or do any manual work during the fifteen years he worked for me, but the workforce he controlled was always managed in a timely way. I had managed to get a good team together and the distribution depot provided a good service to the brand companies within the group.

However, security was always a problem. One day I was surprised to receive a letter from an informant telling me that I had a 'villain', as he described him, working for me as a driver. A second similar letter arrived, but this mentioned chocolates, and I quickly realised these letters were intended for the manager of an adjacent depot which was engaged in distribution of sweets and chocolates, so I passed the letters over to him. This manager initiated enquiries which led to police raiding a driver's house, and lo and behold every conceivable cupboard and wardrobe was filled with Mars Bars and Kit Kats, some in the loft. It took an eight-ton truck to remove the stolen chocolates.

That time it was someone else's problem, but some time later I received a telephone call from an Asian off-licence manager saying that one of my drivers was offering him extra cases of whisky at cut price and adding that he was not the only shop manager who had been made such an offer. With the evidence supplied we identified the driver, but we had to get proof ourselves because the off-licence manager had given the information on the explicit basis that he was not to be involved, and I respected his wish for confidentiality.

We undertook a lot of enquiries and our stock records in the warehouse showed no deficiencies. At this particular depot there were about ten vehicles doing deliveries in a regional area. The loading of vehicles at 6 am was strictly controlled and the rear roller shutter doors were padlocked as the vehicles left the depot and the alarms were activated. However, during a spot check of our suspect's vehicle when it was about to leave the depot one morning, it was found to contain three extra cases, and when questioned he admitted that these had been quickly transferred by him from an adjacent load about to leave the depot. When further questioned he admitted that he had been doing this scam for some time and then selling them to his 'clients'.

Another way of making a quick profit, call it a fringe benefit of the whisky trade, was when full pallet deliveries were made. A driver would delicately remove a case from a middle tier of his pallet. The loss was not detected at the point of delivery as full pallets were offloaded by pallet trucks, and sometimes the missing pallet would remain undetected for days or maybe weeks, so nobody could say with any certainty where the pilfering had taken place – at the Scottish bottle plant, en route or at the regional depot, or maybe at the customer's premises. Scallywag drivers were always up to their tricks.

The answer to all this was to attempt to recruit honest men and women, but there would always be the bad apple seeking his or her opportunity to get rich in an industry where drivers could find a ready market for the odd cases. Shop and pub managers in particular could put illicit bottles through their optics and pocket the cash, and the brewery or owners of the pub would be none the wiser. I'm afraid it was all part of the rich tapestry of the wines and spirits business, and constant vigilance and watertight systems and procedures were an everyday requirement.

However there were aspects of managing driver personnel that turned out to be very rewarding, and some of the good ones really were the 'salt of the earth'. A normal part of man management control within the industry was to produce monthly statistics of vehicle performance to see the comparative productivity of the various drivers. At one particular depot each vehicle had a driver and mate to assist in unloading and also to help with security. However it so happened that one vehicle was always at the top of the league, so to speak. My transport manager thought the world of this particular driver, who was quiet, unassuming and consistent at time keeping; truly, Ron seemed an ideal employee. Then we looked at the driver's mate. John was a big, happy, jovial character and everything he did he did with a smile and very quickly. I had certain thoughts on this issue and told the manager to swap John to a vehicle which was not performing very well. Within weeks its performance had shot up the league, but Ron's had dropped.

By background John had spent years as a dairy farm labourer, but after the death of his farmer, he had been put out of a job and I had recruited him as a driver's mate without an HGV licence. But he was a nice guy and a good influence on other people. If he was told to make a 5 am start, there was never any quibbling.

Having realised his positive influence on other drivers, I immediately sent him at the company's expense to a driving school, so that he could qualify for his HGV. He passed, and soon after he was given his own vehicle. His wages increased by 25% and the benefit to the company was incalculable.

Some years later I held negotiations to introduce single manning of vehicles; John was a great help in accepting the new terms and again he benefited in cash terms from the new working practice. I had many nice people work for me over the years, but John was quite outstanding – he charmed customers wherever he went. Very unfortunately for him, at the age of 62 he had a slight heart attack and was never allowed to drive again for medical reasons.

During these years, the TGWU was ruling with great militancy, the closed shop was a condition of transport operation throughout most of the country and all vehicle deliveries into the brewery trade had to be made by union drivers or they were turned away at customers' premises on shop stewards' instructions. These were nightmare times for transport managers, and most disputes were unofficial strikes, many agitated by politically-motivated flying pickets. Loads were repeatedly being returned to the depot because of unofficial strikes at customers' premises, and I had to deal with many labour-related problems – sometimes as much as a third of my time was concentrated on such matters.

One morning I had a call at home at six o'clock. My transport manager told me six flying picket drivers from a company depot in Liverpool had arrived at 5.30 and were preventing vehicles from going out of or into the depot. They had assembled with placards proclaiming 'T&G OFFICIAL DISPUTE' and they had a steel brazier with a fire burning brightly, warming themselves and boiling water for a brew, a scene often seen outside factories in the seventies. Of course they achieved their aim of stopping 'the job', as they called it.

My first instinct was to ring my colleague in Liverpool

to find out the truth of the matter and ask what six of his employees were doing outside my depot at six o'clock in the morning. Sure enough his depot had been at a standstill for several days and his drivers' shop steward said they were going to make the dispute national. In my experience, many disputes started at Liverpool, and for that reason factory owners avoided it like the plague, such was its reputation for trade union militancy. Cunard and many other shipping companies moved away from Liverpool, and the docks there closed one by one. Formerly there had been eight miles of docks.

Virtually all the disputes were unofficial, so the T&G did not deplete its funds by paying out strike pay to its striking drivers. My Liverpool colleague confirmed that it was an unofficial dispute, so I went to the depot with foreknowledge. When the flying pickets attempted to prevent me from driving on to my site, I told them their signs were wrong, as the dispute was not official. The braziers would be extinguished and removed by my depot staff and the queue of vehicles waiting to come into the depot and those of our own would be expected to leave. I told both our drivers' shop steward and the men who represented the warehousemen that the dispute at Liverpool was clearly an unofficial strike between themselves, and all other company personnel throughout the country were working normally.

I was fortunate to have as my warehouse manager an ex-Merchant Navy officer who was one of the best people managers I ever had, and as it happened, he was a native of Liverpool and knew all the tricks Liverpudlians got up to. These flying pickets were a determined lot and carried on hanging about our main entrance for some time, but I gave an instruction to our warehouse manager that they should not be allowed toilet or tea-making facilities. Another thing in my favour was that our depot was on a privately-owned industrial estate and I had ascertained that they would be regarded as trespassers, so we called the police and had them removed from our works entrance.

About an hour later I got a call from the estate owner, who told me the flying picket drivers had now stopped all vehicles entering the industrial estate, affecting over a hundred traders. The estate owners were upset that I had involved other traders, to which I replied that it was an unofficial dispute and they should do as I had done, ring the police and have them removed. This they did and the flying pickets, having caused mayhem, returned to Liverpool in the afternoon.

Merseyside and the West Midlands were probably the most T&G dominated areas, and of course this was the days of Red Robbo at British Leyland, Longbridge; he and his political conspirators played their part in the de-industrialisation of the West Midlands, but Jack Jones, General Secretary of the T&G, and a series of governments turned a blind eye to what was going on. Industrial legislation at the time allowed such things as flying pickets, closed shops and unofficial disputes to go unhindered. I've forgotten how many times the full-time organiser of the T&G said that if we did not agree his wage demands when the matter was discussed annually he would just shut us down – no thought for the workforce who would lose their jobs. These tinpot union scallywags were left free to cause mayhem throughout the transport industry. Those dates were chaotic times for managers trying to run businesses, and of course many failed. But Mrs Thatcher, a determined leader, came along with labour reform and put an end to this industrial nightmare which had prevailed in the UK for thirty years, and managers could begin to manage their businesses again. I often wonder how present-day managers would have coped with those grim times and the winter of discontent which finally bought things to a head.

It was not just the drivers who were scallywags; I recall that some years earlier I was working in the port of Holyhead, which handled the mail boats and large vessels travelling to Dublin and was also the main route for car travel to Ireland from England, before ro-ro ferries were introduced. This particular dockside installation was managed by the Marine Superintendent, a former army officer, and was quite an important terminal which employed over 200 people. It so happened that a dispute broke out, a typical 'who does what' affair centring on the question of who should tie and untie the ropes which secured the cars to the superstructure of the ship to prevent them moving during the voyage to Dublin, which took about nine hours. Was it the job of the shore staff (dockers), or the ship's marine staff? At that time cars were craned onto the ship and dropped through hatches to two deck levels while the remainder travelled on deck – all had to be made secure by ropes from the car to the ship.

I was part of a small team which was drafted in to hopefully halt this dispute, which had been going on for a week or so. It was a messy affair. Boats were being delayed, some cars not loaded, holidays disrupted. Cars were still being shipped, albeit delayed, but it was costing a fortune in new securing ropes because nobody would untie the ropes at the ports and they were simply cut or slashed by the workforce. About 600 cars were being shipped weekly, and every car needed a new rope.

Before we arrived the management had suggested to the representatives that to settle the dispute, a bonus should be paid for roping each car, and it was agreed that this task would then be part of the shore staff's job. But as a quid pro quo, attention should be given to other working practices. The team was made up of work study men, industrial engineers and rate fixers. Time and motion techniques for work measurement were used; this was seen to be rather controversial, but these were the tools of the trade if schemes were to be constructed. Most of the work was done during the early evening and night, and the two shifts each employed about one hundred men, so at clocking on and clocking off there were a lot of guys around the time office. Our first objective was to find out the work content of the operation to try to ascertain how many bods were required for the various tasks of cargo handling, car movement and handling sacks of mail which travelled up from London and elsewhere on special trains. We knew from the rosters how many were on the payroll, but when trying to observe these characters at clocking on we could not reconcile the headcount at all. We quickly came to the conclusion that a scam was going on, in that men were furtively clocking on two or three of their colleagues. Some came to clock on, then vanished into the darkness and presumably went back to their homes for a good night's sleep. Some would clock on and team up with their observer, then give him the slip to suddenly appear several hours later when he was clocking off. This was quite a large complex covering many acres and there were sheds all over the place with old mattresses so that staff could slumber the night away. It took many months to bring some order to the place.

CHAPTER 5

HIGHWAY ROBBERY

M y experience in Holyhead told me that it wasn't just drivers who could be scallywags – this kind of thing was going on all over the country. There was full employment, but productivity was low as a result of massive work sharing.

There was a common saying in those days that Britain's largest company, ICI, carried more 'passengers' than British Railways. Sadly ICI, because of its bad management, just faded away, its factories taken over mainly by foreign companies, and alas it is no more.

Jumping ahead for a moment in reference to Cert Distribution, the company was dealing mostly in high-value wines and spirits warehousing and distribution, so security of clients' stock was a prime consideration, with daily reconciliation of stock in warehouses a continuous process. Most problems started when the stock left the depot on our transport. All depots from time to time gave us problems, and pilfering was the most problematic area. We had a large depot in South London dealing with maybe 500 clients giving a service for next-day delivery within the M25. We were carrying high-value wines and spirits and tobacco, lots of it vintage champagne, perhaps up to twenty different brands, Moët, Lanson, Perrier etc, and we operated a dozen small vehicles delivering to prestige wine bars, restaurants and hotels. We guaranteed next-day delivery, so the customers held minimal stock at their premises. This depot carried over a thousand wine items, with brands ranging from Blossom Hill to Château Petrus. But things were not going well and we were losing twenty cases of champagne weekly from our fleet of small vehicles, average case value about £300. Drivers were instructed to make sure their vehicles were always alarmed. It was a hazardous business as we knew local villains operating in South London would be following our vans as they left the depot and waiting their opportunity to pounce if a driver did not take care of his load. We had private investigators follow our vans, but nothing was discovered and the champagne kept vanishing.

Eventually we got a lead from our investigator, who observed cars seen near our depot, including a Ford Granada which had been seen on more than one occasion in the proximity of one of our delivery vehicles. It turned out that this scallywag was practising one of the most ingenious scams I ever saw in my many years in the wine and spirits business. This guy had a list of twenty or so hotels and wine bars, mostly in the Mayfair area, and had a comprehensive knowledge of their layout. He had researched their premises and knew their working procedures and the habits of staff and where they stored champagne. He had also got hold of copies of the signatures that might appear on consignment notes.

His modus operandi was to follow a van driver who might be doing twenty calls in the West End. When the driver stopped and was loading say three cases onto his truck, this guy would then nip into the hotel, put on his green porter's dustcoat and wait for the driver to appear, posing as an employee. Then he became quite an actor. He would instruct the driver to put the cases on the floor of reception or wherever, and crack on he was very busy, saying he would put them away later. With a professional flourish he would sign for the goods and the driver would go away, his delivery completed, but as soon as the driver was out of sight the con man would put the cases in his Granada. The whole well-practised operation would be over in thirty seconds – speed was vital to him. The stolen cases might be worth £1000. A scam like this was so easy, especially with the number of transitory hotel staff. This guy obviously thought it was easy money, and ultimately, to avoid a long prison sentence, he owned up to over eighty offences.

Unfortunately, there were drivers among our own staff who would have a go if they thought they had a foolproof plan. We became a little suspicious of a certain driver, as cases were going missing from his vehicle; when he was supposed to be taking a dozen cases to an off-licence, he would only deliver eleven. He knew from experience when an off-licence manager was rather lax and he would pull one across him very quickly.

As a matter of interest it's not always easy to ascertain where pilfering has taken place – whether it was at the original depot, from the vehicle, or at one of the delivery points on the route. Off-licences employ a lot of temporary labour, with late closing hours, and stock often went missing from shops. We were suspicious of one particular guy as there were too many instances of shortage, so much so that we placed a miniature camera at the rear of his vehicle, and it paid off. This driver was in the habit of calling at his home and dropping off a case or two before proceeding on his rounds. He was clearly unaware that he was being photographed as he opened up the rear doors of his van.

We planted micro cameras quite often to catch criminals. A few years earlier at a depot in the North West we were using a subcontractor driver from time to time when we needed to supplement the capacity of our own fleet of vehicles. It was hazardous to use subcontractors, because not all could provide the full insurance cover required for high-value goods. However, this scallywag was able to do so. This incident occurred during the week of Chester Races and his vehicle was loaded for ten or so calls in the North Wales area, including one at the racecourse for the main caterers, who had a very posh marquee for the entertainment of high-flying punters. This particular delivery of thirty cases of champagne was timed for 10.30, but at 11.30 an irate catering manager rang the depot enquiring what had happened to his champagne and explaining that he had a champagne luncheon arranged for one o'clock and only had a few bottles in stock. The depot staff contacted the driver, who was somewhere on the North Wales coast, and he said he had made the delivery to the caterer's tent at Chester

Races at 10.30 as arranged. He was instructed to fax the signed delivery note immediately. This he did, and it was relayed to the catering company. After scrutinizing this signature, they quickly said it did not match any of their staff on duty at 10.30 that morning. To save the company embarrassment we despatched a duplicate consignment to them immediately.

The driver came back to the depot in the early afternoon, showing no sign of guilt. He explained that on arrival at the racecourse shortly after ten o'clock chaos had prevailed and most of the staff appeared to be temps, so he had offloaded the twenty cases and put them inside the marquee, then got one of the guys to sign and proceeded on his way to Wrexham. It all sounded a very plausible story, but the signature issue was bothering us. As we were experienced distributors of high-value goods, it was both the caterers' view and our own that the police should be informed. The driver was then sent on his way to deliver a second load in the area.

The call to the police immediately produced the information that they had had this man under watch a while ago. He had no police record, but they said that in their opinion he was a highly suspicious 'white van driver'. The cases had still not turned up, and the police volunteered to visit his house immediately. When his wife opened the door, they spied down the corridor a single case of champagne, and that was enough for a police search warrant to be issued immediately. At this inspection, the house turned out to be a treasure trove, with many rooms full of goods of all descriptions – food, electrical items of all kinds and yes, our cases of champagne. He was a real scallywag conman, who admitted that when he had seen the chance at the racecourse he had taken it.

Remaining just for a moment in the North West, we had two instances quite different in nature where drivers ended up on the wrong side of the law. On the first occasion a driver was making a delivery to the Midlands of 24 pallets of whisky worth £150,000. This was quite a long story and the emphasis changed many times over the year that followed. At the outset it seemed quite a straightforward case of vehicle hijacking by the criminal fraternity. The driver said he had been travelling south down the M6 in the early morning when he was flagged down by what appeared to be a motorway patrol car and instructed to leave the cab to inspect his rear lights, whereupon he was struck on the head by one of the bogus policemen. The next thing he knew of it was when he regained consciousness several hours later, having been dumped in the field adjacent to the motorway. He hailed a motorist and asked him to take him to the nearest police station.

It was known that there were bogus police cars on the M6 and his story was believed. He had many signs of injury and very bad bruising when examined by the police doctor, and when the police contacted our company for referencing purposes he was given a clean bill of health with no reservations, although the trailer and the 24 pallets were still missing. Nothing more happened for several weeks, and then our burnt-out trailer was found on a disused trading estate in Liverpool – yes, that city again.

As the weeks went by the driver remained off sick with some post-incident nervous issues, and it appeared he would be taking long-term sickness. But that car park tip from the police to keep an eye on the company car park came in handy again, for when this man visited the depot we noted that he was driving quite an expensive car. By now the police were focusing on the driver, and as always when family finances are looked at the first thing was to ascertain the nature of the wife's job, if she had one. When it was discovered that she was a croupier in a Liverpool night club owned by some highly questionable characters, the alarm bells began ringing, so over a period of a month the detectives paid several visits to the club. They found that our driver's car was always parked outside and he was in the bar watching the proceedings until the early hours. What was more, these people were part of the Liverpool underworld and suspected of handling stolen goods.

It didn't take the police very long to rumble the whole thing. The driver admitted to being paid a few thousand pounds for virtually giving the load away (and for his personal injury) and he was to receive a further £5,000 if the crime remained undetected twelve months after its execution. The car park issue revealed itself again, although within the company we had another procedure which should have gone some way to obviate this bogus police hijacking. All our vehicles carried a large cardboard sign which said 'Notice for police – this is a high value load and will follow you to the nearest police station'. This was an integral part of our vehicle security system. Our drivers were instructed never to wind down their windows and certainly not to leave the cab under any circumstances, such was the threat from bogus coppers. This particular man never quite convinced us or the police that he had needed to leave the cab. It lingered on throughout this case. Our scallywag driver had unfortunately been tempted by the get-rich-quick syndrome and keeping some very bad company.

I was only ever involved in one other hijacking, and as always it could have been avoided if procedures had been complied with. The company used to send large loads of spirits to Ireland from a depot close to Liverpool, the destination being a Tesco supermarket in Dublin, and trailers were shipped overnight for deliveries at eight o'clock in the morning. It was a standing instruction not to accept a delivery for a Monday, as there were no sailings on a Sunday night. We preferred to ship Monday, but on this occasion, quite foolishly, our traffic planner booked a Friday night sailing and the management at the depot were unaware of the mistake. However, they realised their error when on Saturday morning the subcontractor rang from Dublin asking where he could park up till Monday. In those days with the 'Troubles' a constant problem the IRA would hijack anything, and they would certainly take a load of Scotch hanging about over Saturday and Sunday. We tried to put the vehicle into a secure park for the weekend, but we did not succeed, and over the weekend the tractor and trailer were stolen. The Gardai said there was no such thing as a secure car park in Ireland and anyway no guard would hang around when the IRA arrived.

Around this time in my career I had responsibility for several depots, and the one near to Merseyside was always throwing up some kind of malpractice or incident. This one had nothing to do with pilfering or missing stock – it was a completely different matter. It so happened that this depot operated as a trunking base for vehicles travelling north to Scotland or south to London, and like most trunking operations they travelled through the night, so a vehicle would leave the North West with a load, travel the 200 miles or so to London, drop his trailer and pick up a trailer intended for the North West. The whole trip would take about nine hours, and we had several trunkers doing this each night.

This again was high value goods, food, wines and spirits, tobacco etc, so we had a procedure which drivers had to follow rigidly, specifying that they were to look after their natural needs within the security of the depot. The procedure stated quite clearly that they had to travel without a break and no stopping until they reached London. This was complied with. They were all relatively young and fit men and the job paid well – there was no shortage of applicants if a vacancy arose. In the interests of better management control we periodically brought in a specialised company which took samples of our tachographs and passed these discs through very precise reading machines, then reported back the results. These readers could give precise information on the driver's performance – virtually every gear change he made, when he turned a corner or when he turned onto a motorway from an A road.

One such spot check on drivers working on the night trunking down to London showed that one driver's performance was different from all the others. He would travel south for a couple of hours and the vehicle would virtually stop, then proceed south for another two hours, then stop again, and then continue to the London depot. There was a similar puzzling sequence of events on the return journey to the North West depot. We initiated an enquiry, checking stock records for shortages, as we thought this man was dropping loose cases out of his cab at pre-arranged drop-off points. The tachograph record revealed that the two locations were motorway service stations, Keele near the Potteries and Canley near Coventry. We continued with our enquiries and got a private detective to follow this vehicle throughout its route to see what the driver was up to. It emerged that this driver was calling in at Keele and picking up a girl, then taking her to Canley. On his way back north several hours later he would call back at Canley and take her back to Keele. When the driver was confronted by the private detective, it turned out that this girl was not his girlfriend but a prostitute, a genuine lady of the night, and he admitted to assisting her for several months; no doubt he was well paid. Apparently for her there was more business in Canley than Keele.

Following this particular experience, I learned that there were very good profits for the girls at motorway stations throughout the nationwide network, and if you think about it, 200 or so sleeper cabs parked up for the night all over the country provide a good market place for the 'ladies of the night'. I think you'll agree that this was a different kind of scallywag, but he had to go.

Returning to matters in South London, it was here that organised crime was most prevalent, in the transport and warehousing industry. Incidents were almost a daily occurrence, and the criminals employed all kinds of tricks to gain rewards for themselves. One such measure was to drive a six-inch nail through a block of wood, then follow the delivery vehicle (usually a light van) to his next delivery point. Whilst the driver was away from the vehicle the block of wood would be placed in front of his rear wheel. The driver would then press on to his next customer completely unaware anything had happened, but a few minutes later he would realise he had a flat tyre. Meanwhile the villains would be following from a safe distance.

What followed was a two-man operation. One man had already left his car (always a stolen vehicle) and was maybe half a mile further up the road ready to assume the role of an innocent bystander. Back at the point of action the driver had left his cab and was examining his flat tyre when along came a man appearing to be a friendly motorist who asked if he could give any assistance, commiserating with him for having the bad luck to get a puncture and telling him there was a telephone box just around the corner. The driver then set off on his walk to find the phone box, but this 'good Samaritan' had already put the phone out of order and would be back with his fellow villain in a minute or so, knowing exactly the state of play, so to speak. Needless to say, both van and contents were gone very quickly and the car and van were found a couple of days later burnt out by a disused dockside warehouse.

This scam was used widely throughout London in the eighties and nineties, so much so that the crime squad issued advice to traders to be aware. The criminal underworld was so active that an organisation was set up by traders to try to reduce the amount of wines and spirits being stolen. I was a director, and I remember being present at a meeting and hearing of a scheme which was particularly daring and bold-faced in its effrontery.

The East End criminal gangs were looking for full loads of whisky travelling overnight from Scotland, and they always had their informers. On this occasion a vehicle carrying a thousand cases of Bells' whisky was going to one of the brewer's depots in the East End. The driver duly turned up having driven through the night from Scotland, and on approaching the entrance gate, only a hundred yards from the depot, he was flagged down by a chap in a supervisor's coat bearing the beer company's logo. This chap told him with great authority to park up on the roadside, as the yard was congested with vehicles, but they would call him in a few minutes. The guy then added that he could get a brew at the rest room inside the depot, and instructed him to book in at reception once he was there, saying 'Don't worry, we'll look after your vehicle'. The driver went for his cup of tea, but when he returned ten minutes later his vehicle was gone, and so was the very convincing 'supervisor'.

Yes, South London was a place full of scallywags, many with evil intent. Having had to deal with whisky thieves and prostitution, we had an incident which involved both drugs and so-called 'drug barons'. Our depot in London, like most of our depots, worked on a twenty-four-hour basis, and usually the night turn was for warehouse staff only who were order picking throughout the night so that we could keep to our next-day delivery service. From time to time we had to supplement our workforce with agency temporary labour, and this was certainly the order of things when peak season Christmas working was introduced, so the staff were not as closely monitored at these times.

It came to my notice that drugs were being circulated on the night shift. Managers indicated to me that they thought a group of people had been seen receiving drugs, albeit for their own use, so we set a trap involving the police to find out how the drugs were getting into the depot. Within a few days of beginning observation an outsider was seen getting into the warehouse via a pedestrian gate which should have been locked at all times, so the police needed to find out who was conspiring with the drug dealer to get him on to the site. A covert police action revealed that one of our temporary staff was the culprit, and we thought that was the end of it. However, under the pressure of police questioning he told us that a drug-dealing gang had got to hear that in a few days' time an order for 900 cases of vodka was to be delivered to an East End brewery, and there was a clear intention by organised criminals to hijack the vehicle and its £100,000 worth of stock.

At the outset the Chief Inspector running this case was keen that we should let the delivery go forward as planned; they would have a number of unmarked squad cars following the goods vehicle on its route and when the vehicle was intercepted by the villains the police, some armed, would move in and arrest all concerned. The police were of course interested in catching some 'Mr Big' from the criminal underground. But the day before the action was to take place, the Chief Inspector called off the whole operation. It was thought someone in the police suddenly got cold feet, maybe because they didn't want to be seen conspiring with a company in order to catch some real criminals. Needless to say the 900 cases of vodka never left the depot and the order was fulfilled from another source. London was always the stronghold of villains in the wines and spirits industry.

Some significant load security devices came onto the market in the 1970s to protect loaded trailers from being stolen by a rogue trailer unit, and the fitting of clamps on to the trailers' connectors stopped rogue tractors stealing loaded trailers standing in hauliers' yards because the clamps would not allow the tractor to couple to a trailer. Curtain-sided trailers, parked or travelling, were always a target for the petty thief with his Stanley knife ready to slash and steal a few cases, but he found it impossible after our curtain-sided trailers and wagons were fitted with steel mesh reinforced curtains.

The big boys in the criminal world in the big cities could not have operated if there had not been a market of small dishonest traders willing to accept stolen goods. In fact a load of 1,500 cases would be hijacked to order to satisfy the needs of these people, perhaps as many as 50 shopkeepers taking 30 cases each, and Mr Big would have a distribution network which could get rid of the whole lot in two or three days. But it wasn't always controlled by the hijacker; the retail and transport trade were inherently dishonest in some areas. I remember the sad case of a very old and well-established haulage company whose owner listened to siren voices and agreed to get involved in a scam. As a haulier well known in the trade for bringing loads of scotch into the South of England, this man was approached by what you might call a consortium of small shopkeepers who between them had agreed to take the 1200 cases. The leader of this band of off-licence operators suggested that ways could be found to let one of the loads parked at his depot be removed overnight. This particular load was due at our depot first thing in the morning, but almost immediately the haulier rang the depot manager and informed him that someone had stolen the trailer overnight. The police immediately set in motion steps to investigate. The haulier became a little anxious when told his yard perimeter alarm and arc lamps had been deactivated, and this particular trailer had not been close-parked with others – close parking of trailers prevents hijacking. The police looked into the financial side of the business and saw that there were some hefty finance bills due on some new vehicles.

This man was arrested quite soon and quickly sent to Winson Green prison in Birmingham for three years, along with a motley crew of small shopkeepers. I had been doing business with him for three years and was amazed that he should have been taken in by such a scheme. This man had worked hard for twenty years and still drove a vehicle daily, yet he had succumbed to temptation like a common criminal. His going to jail had a profound effect on his family, and I think this particular happening was one of the most regrettable human experiences I remember.

Not all scallywags are men. I remember speaking to the manager of a large department store which was losing a good deal of stock, apparently through shoplifting by customers. They brought in a security company to carry out a full examination of the losses and were very surprised to learn that most of the stolen stock was down to their own workforce, which was largely female. In this context a spate of petty losses was discovered at our depots in the South of England. It became clear that the responsibility for the losses was very much a Scottish bottling plant problem, so I travelled up to Scotland and spent a few days with the production managers at several bottling plants. It was clearly understood that they had a constant petty thieving problem, as they kept finding bottles with contents three or four inches below the correct level, or half a dozen miniatures would be missing from a case, or maybe a single bottle was missing from a case of twelve. Petty things, but very annoying to the legitimate customer, so pressure fell on the bottling plants to stop this petty pilfering by the women on the overwhelmingly female production lines. It has to be understood that by the nature of their employment in the drinks business there were a fair number of alcoholics in the industry. The historic availability of the dram allowance, which stopped the production line in the morning and again in the afternoon to allow all staff to consume a small glass of whisky, might have been the cause of some of them becoming alcoholics. In an attempt to reduce pilfering, management introduced random searches of personnel at close of work to catch the culprits.

A favourite method to smuggle stock off site was for a woman to tie a piece of string around a bottle and suspend it between her legs, hidden by her skirt as she walked off site among some 2000 employees. Another favourite trick was to conceal miniatures in an oversized bra, which was a ruse usually used by the larger ladies.

Despite the introduction of these random searches, bottles continued to go missing. Some employees employed a method of pilfering which was much harder to detect. These people, 'dram merchants' as we called them, didn't take stock off site – they drank it at work. When the bottles were travelling down the production line, they would quickly twist the top off one, take a large swig and put the bottle back. Yes, these ladies were scallywags to match any man.

That reminds me of a real scallywag I had met back in my teens. Next to the farm I lived on in my early teens was a sewage farm, run by the local water board and dealing with the effluent from a nearby housing estate. It had just one employee, Bill, the site manager, who controlled all activities that went on there. It was a rather mysterious establishment on the edge of the village and as long as the smell was kept to a minimum, nobody cared too much about what went on inside.

My father had a milk round, and my Saturday job was to visit customers to collect their money for eggs and milk he had supplied to them. Bill's house was on the milk round. He did not work Saturdays, but it turned out he had a sideline which was very closely related to his day job, and as a young teenager I was about to see what it was. One Saturday when I called for his milk money, I found a small queue of people waiting to see him in his back kitchen. I entered to see an array of false teeth laid out in order of size on the table. These people were trying them on for size, ably assisted by Bill. It seemed incredible to me. In the 1950s it was quite common for people to have all their teeth removed to be replaced by false teeth (my father was one of them). These people I saw being fitted up with a replacement pair didn't seem in the least embarrassed at seeing each other's plight.

You may well ask where these teeth came from. It seems that after a night of indulgence, usually on a Friday or Saturday, people became sick, and when visiting the lavatory their teeth, along with everything else, were flushed away along a circuitous route of drains to Bill's sewage farm some two miles away. When Bill turned up for work on Monday, there was always a ready supply caught in the griddle. This was quite a lucrative sideline. He didn't know anything about marketing, but he could see a business opportunity when it presented itself!

Enough of the scallywags I have come across. I return now to life in the West Midlands. On the domestic front, although we were not Catholics we sent our son Paul to a convent primary school. It was fee-paying, but its success rate in the Eleven Plus exam was one of the highest in the West Midlands. Quite remarkably, Sister Bridget had been head teacher for fifty years and even after all those years she demanded excellence from her staff to get the best results for her pupils, despite never accepting any wages or salary; she lived in the convent with the other nuns. Her whole life was dedicated to educating children and her only reward was hearing of the subsequent success of her pupils.

At this stage I should point out that about a year after starting Paul at the Convent Prep School we moved house, so he went to a local primary school for a year or so. I noticed that his early promise had not been sustained, so Pat and I agreed that he should return to the Convent. However, after giving him a short test Sister Bridget was reluctant to take him back, and she laid down the condition that we should enrol him at the local Poetry Society branch for Saturday coaching to try to eradicate the 'Brummie' accent he had acquired in the past year. She was very cross with us. She said he had learned virtually nothing in the past year, and almost accused us of ruining his education. Furthermore she insisted that we should strictly supervise the homework she would set for him for the next six months. After this episode we were very much in awe of Sister Bridget and her 'spare the rod and spoil the child' policy. There was no doubt that he methods were very successful, and when she passed away many years later the church was filled with professional people of all ages who had once been her pupils.

Without any special coaching, Paul passed the examination for King Edward's School, Birmingham, which at that time was one of the finest direct grant grammar schools in the UK, with some famous old boys as such as J R R Tolkien of *Lord of the Rings*, Field Marshall Sir William Slim of Burma of Second World War fame, the politician Enoch Powell and the TV personality Bill Oddie.

As a matter of interest, Enoch Powell came of parents of quite modest background, but he turned out to be one of the most brilliant academic scholars of his time, getting a double first at Trinity College Cambridge, then serving in the army in the Second World War in the Desert Campaign. He became one of the youngest brigadiers in the army. He spoke seven languages, including Welsh, being a native Welshman. As the Conservative MP for Wolverhampton he was something of a seer. He made speeches which at the time were attacked as racist, predicting dire consequences in the future for unchecked immigration into the UK, although he had huge public support. Today we can see the truth in his predictions. Classical historians like Powell always said there has never been a harmonious multi-cultural society. In retrospect I guess they were more interested in culture and religion than race.

The social mobility that direct grant schools gave to bright children from poor families was destroyed by the Blair government for political reasons and today King Edward's has fallen massively in the league tables because it no longer takes in the brightest and best children. It is no longer a bastion of educational excellence in the Midlands, giving the opportunity for working-class boys from the area to go to Oxford or Cambridge.

At the time when Paul was at King Edward's School the Chief Master's name was Fisher, and he ruled the school with a rod of iron. On one occasion Pat and I had to attend a weekend conference in London. We intended to take Paul away from the school on the Friday afternoon and mentioned this to the school, saying he would in any case only be playing rugby. The immediate reply was that we should reconsider this and in any case that we should talk to Mr Fisher first. Fisher immediately told us that he was rejecting our written request, saying that if we were so ill-advised as to remove Paul from the school, he would not be re-admitted on the Monday. He reminded us that there was a long waiting list for Paul's place. We were quite dumbfounded. Fisher regarded rugby as a very important team sport, as important as the academic curriculum. Needless to say we made other arrangements for our weekend. Kenneth Clarke, the then Chancellor of the Exchequer, had a son in the same class as Paul, and he too had to abide by Fisher's rules. I wonder how parents today would react to this kind of regime.

Overall Paul benefited from an excellent education and went on to university to read law, eventually gaining a position with a large London practice.

Around this time I was surprised one day to receive an invitation to join the Justices' Bench at Dudley, our nearest large town. I was in my late thirties at the time and it seemed they were looking for people of that age who had reached relatively senior positions in industrial life. The only problem was that you had to be available for court sittings for one day each fortnight. My employers told me that they were not prepared for me to away from my office so regularly, so I declined the invitation. It was obviously the right decision, for before the year was out I found I would now be expected to spent more time in the south of England. I'm not sure on reflection whether my social views would have been acceptable to other bench members anyway.

By this time I was in my late forties and one day I read a headline in the national press which took me back to my RAF intelligence work in Bad Eilsen, Germany, back in 1955. The papers carried the story that Geoffrey Prime, an ex-RAF serviceman at RAF Gatow in Berlin, had been convicted of spying for the KGB and the Lord Chief Justice had sentenced him to jail for 38 years. I reflected on the work that we in the intelligence secretariat in the British zone had done, so closely connected by the air corridor into RAF Gatow, and this man Prime had joined the team in intelligence. He was a signaller and linguist in Russian and we had many people like him, because in those days, just a few years after the end of the war, many people were attempting to get from east to west, some of them KGB agents trying to get into Western Europe.

We tried through the work of MI6 to protect our eastern sources, ie people spying for us, but they were always under threat from the KGB and other Warsaw Pact intelligence services. So the KGB had been successful in turning Prime into one of their agents while he was working at RAF Gatow, and he had successfully kept his Soviet associations throughout the time he was working in Berlin. Knowing how tight security was in RAF intelligence, I was amazed that he could have got away with it for five years whilst in Berlin, and what's more he left the RAF without being detected. He continued spying for the KGB and managed to get classified intelligence jobs in London and at the new GCHQ in Cheltenham, where he worked for years before leaving, still undetected. He was only found out when information became available about him assaulting young girls, because when police were searching his house near Worcester for evidence of paedophilia they also, quite by accident, found considerable evidence in the loft that he had been a Russian agent for decades. It was hard to believe that he had got through the positive vetting procedure and continued for so long undetected.

I was now very much in the groove at work, and no longer having to pay school fees. Distillers was a good employer and I felt no need to look around for alternative employment. However in 1975, after we had lived at Kingswinford for a few years, I felt the urge to move further into the countryside, and Pat and I spent a lot of time looking around for a larger detached house, perhaps with an acre of land to give us some space. I suppose my farming background drove me towards country living again. Eventually we found the right property, Stratford House in the idyllic black and white village of Claverley in Shropshire, some ten miles from my place of work. It was a big step up in financial terms, but I managed to pay for it using funds I had acquired from disposing of a second property I had had built in Cheshire. The background to this was that before disposing of my Cheshire house in 1970, I had fenced off part of the rear garden to create a building plot on which I built another house. I rented this out for some time, but when I needed the capital for the Claverley house the extra cash was crucial. We eventually lived in that house for 38 years. It was set in an acre of land, which was ideal for our newly-acquired Labrador.

While we were there we joined in with village life. Pat joined the local amateur dramatic society, which was considered of a high standard, and was successful in drama competitions at Ludlow and Worcester and such places. At this time, because I was in the drinks trade, we held Pimms parties for several years to raise money for selected charities. We could accommodate fifty or so people from the village quite easily in our large garden and these parties became quite an occasion. In those days village parties were a feature of village life, and I well remember a humorous episode when we had a party at our house and Pat of course was the hostess. She was flitting between kitchen and dining room as she served the different courses, but nevertheless she managed to keep up with the conversations of the guests. Among them were a retired stockbroker, Gerry Devine, and his wife. Gerry had a tendency to dominate the conversation and on this occasion he was getting a bit too much for Pat. She interrupted him in full flow, looked him in the eye and said "Gerry, please be quiet, you're acting like a senile delinquent". This brought a howl of laughter from the other guests, but that was Pat, she didn't suffer fools gladly. Gerry was no fool, and he was not offended by this interjection – in fact he thought it was rather funny. Ever afterwards he would introduce as Pat as 'this young lady who thinks I'm a senile delinquent'. I think he rather liked the title. She certainly had quick wit and a neat turn of phrase, probably as a result of being an avid reader – she reckoned she had read over three thousand books.

Life with Distillers continued to be very settled and our social life was enjoyable, with the company providing little sweeteners to keep its management onside, and wives were invited to join us on weekend conferences at top London venues.

Once when attending a white tie dinner party with thirty or so people, Pat happened to be sitting next to the wife of Peter Whitley, the boss of Johnnie Walker. Mrs Whitley was maybe twenty years older than Pat. She had been a childhood friend of the young princesses Elizabeth and Margaret and has subsequently been a bridesmaid at the Queen's wedding. Quite remarkably, she had spent part of her early childhood living in a large manor house in our village of Claverley, so there was plenty for them to chat about. Afterwards she had moved down to London when her father had become Marquess of Cambridge, so her title was Lady Mary Cambridge. She died a few years ago, and I think it is right to say that Prince William could not adopt the title of Duke of Cambridge until after the death of Lady Mary.

I mentioned meeting Lady Mary to some of the older residents of Claverley one day and they said they could well remember the royal train coming to Wolverhampton and the former Queen Mary travelling into the village to visit Lady Mary, her godchild, in the 1930s when they lived at Dallicote Manor. I know the former owner of this house and he tells me he knew nothing of the royal connection.

I remember attending the Institute of Transport annual ball at the Dorchester, which entailed an overnight stay there. Having taken afternoon tea, we were taking the lift to our room when a small swarthy-looking man got into the lift with us on the ground floor. Pat and I paid him little attention and he got out of the lift before us. As the lift continued, the lift attendant remarked that we had just been travelling with one of the richest men in the world – the Sultan of Brunei. A couple of years later the Sultan actually bought the Dorchester. He appeared quite an insignificant person, with none of the trappings of great wealth. In fact he and his retinue occupied virtually a whole floor when he visited.

Another feature of that dinner and ball was the social mix of the 300 guests. Only a couple of days before, Ray Buckton, who was the General Secretary of the ASLEF, the train drivers' union, had been leading his union into a national strike. He was a very left-wing trade union leader, the last man you would have expected to see at a black tie evening at the best hotel in London, hobnobbing with the rich and powerful and apparently enjoying the high life with after-dinner brandies and cigars. I often wondered what his members would have thought of his double lifestyle. It seemed a little strange to me then, but in later years I got used to trade union leaders and politicians with their double standards. In fact in 2009, long after my retirement, I submitted some suggestions about MPs' pay and benefits to the Commission on Standards in Public Life.

Sir Christopher Kelly, who was in charge of the Commission, was quite impressed by my submission and wrote to me asking if he could give my pages wider circulation, including to MPs. I gave him my permission to do so – I have never had a high opinion of MPs anyway, although I could get on with chaps like Ken Clarke, who I mentioned earlier. A few years earlier I remember having a drink with him at Bridgnorth Conservative Club when he was drumming up support for himself in trying to become Leader of the Conservative Party while they were in opposition. At the time he was a director of BAT, British American Tobacco. He lost the leadership contest to Ian Duncan Smith, a political lightweight if ever there was one, certainly compared to Ken, who had held all the senior cabinet posts in the Thatcher governments – a foretaste of the future of the Conservative Party, if one was needed.

Ken was a comfortable dresser, but his chalkstripe double-breasted suit was right out of Saville Row and his suede brogues looked like Church's to me. All reports of him walking around in Hush Puppies were pure fabrication, I think.

Although the Distillers Company was an excellent company to work for, it also seemed to be a somewhat controversial organisation because of its connection with the thalidomide scandal back in the 1960s, and maybe because it did not necessarily face up to its responsibilities in the matter. There was widespread public action against the company with demonstrations, marches and the like, just at the time when the IRA was at its most active, carrying out various terrorist atrocities. It so happened that Pat and I, along with twenty or so others, led a weekend DCL seminar at the Box Hill Hotel in Dorking. The event was run on the usual lines with sessions on Friday and Saturday and winding up with a black-tie dinner on the Saturday evening. The Box Hill is quite a large hotel and maybe a couple of hundred people were on the premises on the Saturday evening. Suddenly at about 10 pm the hotel alarm bells started ringing – it was a bomb alert. Everyone had to decant into the hotel car park while the official and police searched the bedrooms etc for a bomb. It was quite a scary interlude, and it went on for an hour or so. The ladies were not best pleased, as they had to stand around outside in their flimsy evening gowns. One of our party, Don Rowe, always a comical character, came to the rescue by producing a ukulele from the boot of his car without prompting proceeded to go through his entire repertoire of George Formby songs, starting with 'When I'm Cleaning Windows'. Don was a great mimic and entertainer. To start with his performance was just for our little party, when others saw what was going on, he continued by doing a few Vera Lynn oldies. The gathering soon forgot all about the bomb scare. Some people were having such a good time singing and dancing that when it was eventually declared to be a false alarm, they were reluctant to go back inside. Don could certainly have pursued an alternative career! Sadly though, years later he was made redundant, and fortunately I was able to offer him a position. He was a nice guy. It's surprising how people's lives and careers can be intertwined.

Because I was a professional transport man and served on several trade committees, I had many invitations to functions in various places and one of these, sponsored by an international transport company, was a weekend transport seminar held at Magdalen College, Oxford. The evening commenced with drinks in the Oscar Wilde study room at Magdalen. I was intrigued to see his room, which was so big that sherry was served there to over 80 people. Wilde must certainly have had a privileged life there. I enjoyed this annual event, which included a black tie dinner in the banqueting hall with after-dinner guests speakers. This was an annual event at Magdalene for several years, and on one occasion I sat next to the great cricketer Fred Trueman, who was the guest speaker.

Away from our work-related social life, Pat and I contrived to afford a couple of cruises on the QE2. It was in those early days before cruising became a mass market, and life on the ship was most enjoyable once you got out of Southampton Water. I say that because this was the era of the lightning strike and on our first cruise we got caught up in one such dispute, having travelled from our home completely unaware of what we were running into. On arriving at the ocean terminal where travellers parked their cars, we were told to park and leave our car keys with an attendant and proceed onto the gangway and into the ship for some complimentary drinks. Some time later we were informed over the ship's Tannoy system that an industrial dispute had arisen and that accordingly our departure would be delayed for an indeterminate period. We waited around for hours until this unofficial dispute was settled, and only then could our cases be brought onto the ship.

Eventually it turned into a very enjoyable little episode. Pat loved the quite formal evening dining arrangements and the dancing which followed. We made a lot of friends, and being still quite young we would dance on until the early hours. I remember Joe Loss and his band providing the music. He was a top man at the time, and he always finished with his signature tine, 'In the Mood'.

One evening I was involved in a funny interlude in the Queen's Ballroom just after Joe and his men had departed. As we were leaving with friends I took a close look at the Steinway piano on the stage, and Pat suggested I should have a go on it, 'just for fun'. I sat down and started to play In the Mood from memory, followed by a few other songs I knew, and quite amazingly the lingering cruisers took to this as I played for them. Pat took a photograph of me at the keyboard. It was an opportunity too good to miss for me and we often recalled it in later years.

For a period of thirty years or so from the 1960s to the 80s, successive governments, whether Conservative or Labour, could only govern with the agreement of the Trades Unions and their politically-motivated shop stewards and the power wielded by such union bosses as Hugh Scanlon, Jack Jones and Clive Jenkins repeatedly brought the country to a standstill and led in large measure to the de-industrialisation of the British economy. The Attlee government after the war was stuffed with fellow travellers and icons such as Bertrand Russell and George Bernard Shaw and a host of university dons were somehow transfixed by the communism theory, so activists in the trade unions were given full rein within our industries to cause as many problems as they could.

Eventually it all culminated in the 'winter of discontent' in 1978-9 and the electorate threw the Labour government out. Thatcher replaced Callaghan and set about a programme to legislate to reduce the power of the unions. It took years, and by then we had lost huge swathes of industry to the Continent, Japan and others.

When you consider that in 1950 the UK had 15% of the world's production and we have managed over the years to reduce that to just 1%, you realise how far we have fallen. But one country, Russia, has done even worse. No wonder in 1989 the Russian people rejected communism and started to introduce free enterprise systems into their economy. On a recent visit to Russia I was told that over 40 million Russians were killed in what they called the 'reign of terror' during the revolution of Lenin and Stalin. Whilst travelling through the countryside I noticed many Russians working on Saturdays and was told by a Russian traveller that the six-day working week still applied to their workforce and for the peasants working in the countryside, their lifestyle was little better than it had been in 1917. We fared much better, having enjoyed a five-day week for nearly seventy years, but the moral of all this is that you should see and travel for yourself – don't listen to the ideological claptrap of people like Russell, whose views as imparted to students in the 1940s were, in the light of experience and history, badly mistaken.

It was pointed out to us that the peasants still have a very hard life. In the most difficult times in their extreme winters little heating is provided in their homes and they can only keep warm by putting on more clothes, sometimes as many as eight layers, and nobody baths during the long, cold winter. In fact many houses do not have running water. Lenin's revolution did not benefit these people.

But enough of my experiences and thoughts of post-war industrial Britain. Returning to our social life, around that time I was invited to join a social club called 51 International, an organisation similar to Round Table. We had evening meetings with dinner twice a month and always had an after-dinner speaker, and a principal activity within the organisation was community service and fundraising for local charities. It was a men's club and there were many clubs within the West Midlands to be visited, but the ladies were also invited to several social events, including an annual ladies' evening. It provided a good social life, and because of its international origins in Waterloo, Belgium, there were many weekend charter visits to the Continent. It was a principal that hotels were not used, so you were matched with similar families in Belgium over there and on return visits to England, so we got to know many Continentals. This ensured that exchange visits for children were arranged. Our son Paul was starting to learn French at the time, and it was particularly useful for learning foreign languages.

We had quite an exciting social life for several years and it only came to an end when I eventually took a job based in London some time later. One thing that did not sit square with me was that although we were all management types or professional people, in comparison with our Belgian friends we were certainly the poor relations. They had progressed rapidly in those post-war years from being a terribly defeated nation only two decades before in the 1950s.

Around this time, because we had a long-term need to pay school fees, Pat returned to the bank in a part-time capacity to help us to eke things out. Our financial budgeting became quite tight, but we did like to get away for at least one week in the summer holidays, perhaps to Bournemouth, Newquay or Torquay. We did not venture to southern Europe, but holidaying in England was expensive enough because we liked to go to a good hotel.

One year in Torquay we were induced to buy a week's time share at the Osborne Hotel. We had just paid nearly a thousand pounds for a week in a Torquay hotel, so to pay £2500 for a hundred years did not seem such a bad deal! So started our relationship with the Osborne, which lasted for over 30 years. In those early years before Paul went up to university we always used our time share week there, but later we would often swap it, sometimes for places on the Continent but more often America. In fact we had a love affair with the USA in the 1980s, travelling to perhaps a dozen different holiday centres, and on each occasion our trip was over two weeks. We were fortunate in having our time share at the Osborne because at that time the Americans were so eager to come to England that we were always able to swap our week there for two weeks in the States. A further bonus was that we always got accommodation for four or six people over there, so we could take friends or family with us.

Our first trip entailed a flight into Washington followed by a hire car journey into Virginia and a week's stay in the Appalachians. Afterwards we drove north for about a thousand miles through New York State and New Hampshire, to a second week in Stowe in Vermont close to the Canadian border, and then tracked south to Boston where we spent a few days before flying home from Logan Airport. Timeshare certainly opened our horizons, and because we always travelled independently, planning our own routes, we met many great Americans, who always seemed so friendly. It was there we became acquainted with the massive size and obesity of Americans, who quite commonly needed special wide chairs to sit on. On one occasion we were dining at a place some twenty floors up, occupying a beautiful view across Boston Harbour where the famous Boston Tea Party had taken place a couple of hundred years before, when two of the fattest ladies I have ever seen took the next table to us – our table was next to the windows. There were four in our party and our male guest, who had a great sense of humour, leaned over to me and whispered in my ear that I should move away from the window because if one of the ladies broke wind I might find myself flying out of it. He clearly thought I was in mortal danger.

We had some very enjoyable times in the USA, although being such a big country you had to travel many miles to get a flavour of the place. Strangely enough people from different states were quite insular in their approach to their fellow Americans and rarely travelled outside their own state. When we talked about travelling two or three thousand miles overland in two or three weeks they were quite amazed and would ask us what the other states were like, although we had only seen them as visitors.

It was a place of great contrasts, and in those days New York was a place where violence could break out without warning. On one occasion following a week in Cape Cod where we were visiting hotspots associated with the Kennedy clan, we the travelled due west, crossing the mighty Hudson river and travelling on to the Pocono Mountains in Pennsylvania for a second week at a golf resort. While we were there my travelling friend, who had been a boxing enthusiast for years, persuaded me to go to a boxing match which was being held in an arena at the resort. All was going well until in one of the bouts a black boxer was disqualified for low hitting. All kinds of missiles were thrown into the ring, and quite suddenly it was filled with supporters of the two boxers, all laying into each other. The disqualified fighter would not leave the ring, and suddenly a massive policewoman jumped into the ring. She sat on him and with her great weight pinned him to the ground until he was handcuffed, then she dragged him out of the ring, after which a semblance of order was regained. By now two white English guys among the sea of black faces had thought it wise to make a quick departure.

The following day we travelled to New York, where we spent four days in Manhattan, staying at the Crown Plaza Hotel on Broadway, adjacent to 42nd Street. Quite amazingly I found driving in Manhattan not as difficult as I'd been told it would be, but even so I abandoned the hire car on day one. At reception, I requested a room no higher than the tenth floor as I had never been one for heights, but was told the rooms did not start until you reached the 25th floor. As we were visitors they had reserved two rooms for us on the 47th floor. Apart from sleeping I spent most of the day at ground level.

One morning while I was just killing time I took a stroll out in the direction of Times Square, which was maybe a hundred yards away, and noticed a car parked on Broadway at a set of traffic lights. Immediately a police car drew up behind and a policeman asked the offending driver to move on as he was causing a traffic hazard. I watched from just a few yards away. The car driver, by way of explanation, said his buddy was collecting a take-away from an adjacent diner and he would only be a minute or so. Without waiting for any more explanation the policeman grabbed him by the throat, dragged him clear of his car, threw him on the bonnet, handcuffed him and dumped him in the back of the police car. Then he whistled for a tow truck and drove off with this guy in the back. Almost immediately a tow truck appeared and within moments the offending vehicle was gone. A couple of minutes later the guy with the take-away showed up and started looking up and down Broadway. I volunteered the information that his friend had been arrested and the car had been taken away in the direction of Greenwich Village.

Yes, violence broke out very quickly in New York in those days. You just had to keep your head down. We were advised that as tourists we should not use the subways and should only use taxis vetted and nominated by the hotel. This warning also applied to Boston with its American-Irish contingent, who were very anti-English.

The most blatant show of violence occurred as we were waiting in the taxi rank in the basement of our hotel on our departure to Kennedy Airport. Immediately in front of us were two Japanese men holding onto their suitcases and waiting for a cab. I had already noticed that the cab drivers never got out of their cars, just letting the bell boy in his Crown Plaza uniform stow the cases in the boot and pick up the tips. When it came to the turn of the two Japanese, the bell boy told them to put their cases on the ground and get in the taxi. One of the men held onto his case and attempted to get into the cab with it, at which point the bell boy punched him very violently in the face and the blood flowed freely. He then proceeded to bundle him into the taxi with his friend and signalled for the taxi to depart.

It was then our turn, and I well remember very distinctly saying to Dennis, 'For goodness sake don't touch those cases whatever you do'. I was glad to give the guy a few dollars and get away unharmed. Yes, New York was a city where violence could break out at the drop of a hat, but away from the metropolitan areas you felt completely safe, and that was where we spent most of our time.

Strangely enough, Washington was a place where one had to be very careful, always making sure all the car windows were closed when approaching traffic lights, because gangs of black men were hanging around waiting to snatch your property or even pull careless tourists out of their cars. If you were not careful you get mugged two hundred yards from the White House. Parts of New Jersey were also black spots for crime. I recall spending a night in a motel there and being told by the guy in reception to always keep the door closed and locked with a security chain in place. He also advised us not to spend 'over long' in the bar, so we were glad we were only spending one night in this prison-like motel. The following morning when paying the bill I commented that the bedroom door was made of solid steel, and he replied that if they were made of wood someone with an axe could break in during the night. Yes, one night was enough in that part of New Jersey.

We certainly did get value for money from that week of timeshare, and it opened up a series of interesting and adventurous holidays, in the Carolinas, the Midwest and elsewhere. Perhaps our longest trip followed the time we flew into Houston Texas. We stayed the first week at a resort a hundred miles north of Houston. The flight out of Heathrow was delayed by two hours because some bright spark, having checked in his luggage, then decided not to travel, so we had been travelling for 24 hours by the time we finally arrived at our destination a couple of miles from Dallas. After a few days there we decided to cut short our stay in Texas because we had heard on the weather forecast that a hurricane was heading for Galveston just a short distance away, and our ultimate destination was Tampa in Florida some two thousand miles away, given the detours we intended to make. Our next destination was New Orleans, a substantial drive away, but unfortunately Hurricane George was now forecast to make landfall somewhere on the Louisiana coast and we were heading in that general direction.

We reached New Orleans after driving for hours through heavy rain, spent a few hours there and saw the sights but decided to press on. New Orleans sticks out into the Gulf of Mexico, so we had to travel east out of the city on an elevated concrete highway suspended above the raging ocean. Fortunately we were in a big Lincoln town car and we drove without stopping for over four hours, travelling through Mississippi towards our next destination, Biloxi, Alabama. I can tell you the car was very silent during that drive.

Fortunately the main road was built on piles in anticipation of flooding, but the side roads to left and right were completely flooded. We could not drive too fast as even the big Lincoln was prone to aquaplaning and we saw several cars virtually submerged at the side of the road. But the wind and rain gradually subsided and we stopped at Biloxi for a few days. Biloxi turned out to have many offshore hotels, renowned for gambling, a sort of poor man's Las Vegas. We had to make a detour around Mobile because the underpasses were still full of water, but it wasn't a place of great interest so we pressed on towards Tallahassee and the Florida Panhandle, as they call it, and finally found solace at a delightful resort called Distin, where from the resort lounge you could walk straight out onto the beach. The sand was as white as driven snow and the water was comfortably warm. However after a night's stay we headed east towards our final destination, the upmarket resort of Sarasota on the Gulf of Mexico north of Fort Myers and the renowned Sanibel Island. Two days later we left our Lincoln behind and flew back from Tampa.

After doing a lot of motoring in the States, I came to the conclusion that the Americans are the best civil engineers in the world. They have built their network of roads very much with the user in mind and their achievements in building highways and bridges across vast rivers and bays was quite amazing. The ocean highway across Chesapeake Bay and the high-rise bridge over the bay at St Petersburg are amazing constructions.

Our second trip to America began in Florida, where we flew into Orlando and stayed at the renowned Orange Lakes Country Club. From there we spent a couple of days in Disneyland and then for our second week we travelled north through Florida into Georgia to a resort north of Atlanta, again on a golf course. Our travelling companions were golf enthusiasts, so we played a few rounds there.

Atlanta is the home of Coca Cola, so we thought we would have a look around the place. We were given the historical background to the best-known company in the world, and were then taken to a sampling room for a complimentary drink. When the PR man commented that everyone had of course drunk Coca Cola, my friend put his hand up and replied that he had not. The man was aghast that anyone could have reached the age of 60 without drinking his product. That was a highly amusing incident.

The Atlanta of *Gone With The Wind* fame had now become a big modern city, and an eight-lane highway went straight through it heading north for Tennessee. We stayed in Georgia for a week and then headed east, for we were both golf enthusiasts and wanted to see the Augusta

Club. Rather sadly however, we were barred from entering, so we then ploughed on towards the Atlantic for a two-day stop at Savannah, quite an historic place for the Americans. It gained its notoriety for being one of the principal towns of the slave trade, and you could tell from the layout that this had been a very prosperous place two or three hundred years ago. It was now a bustling seaport and cruise ships stopped there on days out from New York, on the way down to Palm Beach. We dined at the Pink Room, perhaps the best restaurant in Savannah, just a stone's throw from the place where the film *Forrest Gump* was shot. Then we travelled south to Daytona Beach, scene of various land speed record attempts, had lunch at a beach restaurant and then pressed on down to Orlando for the flight back to Heathrow. A highlight of that trip was having dinner at Jimmy Carter's favourite place and watching the sun go down over the Georgia hills. You can tell from all this that our little investment in the Osborne Hotel made a major impact on our lives for ten years or so.

The author as a two-year-old, 1937

Mother and father before marriage, aged 24

The author aged 6 at Poplar Farm, Daresbury

The author aged 12 in the orchard at Bleak House Farm

Aged 15 – in my first suit

My wedding to Patricia in 1961, with her parents

As groomsman at my sister's wedding, 1965

Aged 11, in the first form at Rudheath School (right, bottom row)

5 Flight, RAF Melksham 1953 (author is 4th from left, middle row)

Flight commanders, with the dreaded Corporal Dalton top right

With the family Humber Hawk, 1958

At a conference with senior managers and directors of the Distillers Company Ltd

Pat and me with the family at the Spring Garden night club, Naples, Gulf of Mexico

With Pat and Paul at his graduation day, 1989

Stratford House, Shropshire, our family home for 38 years

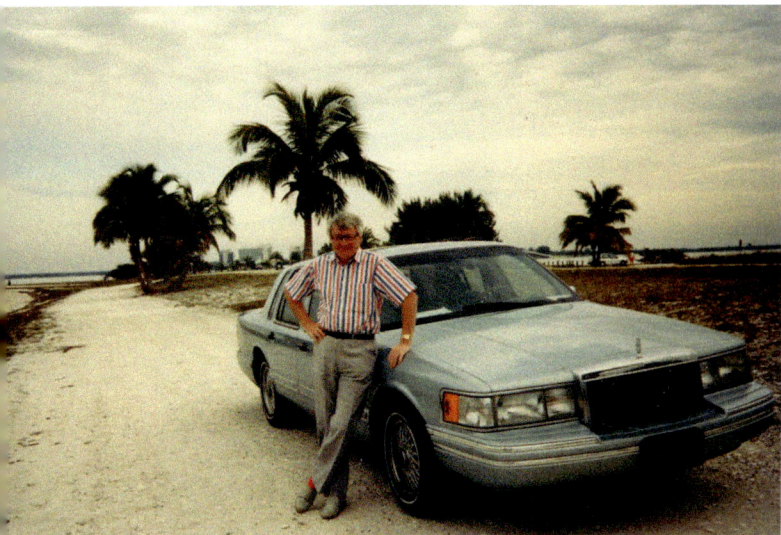

With a Lincoln car on Sanibel Island, Florida

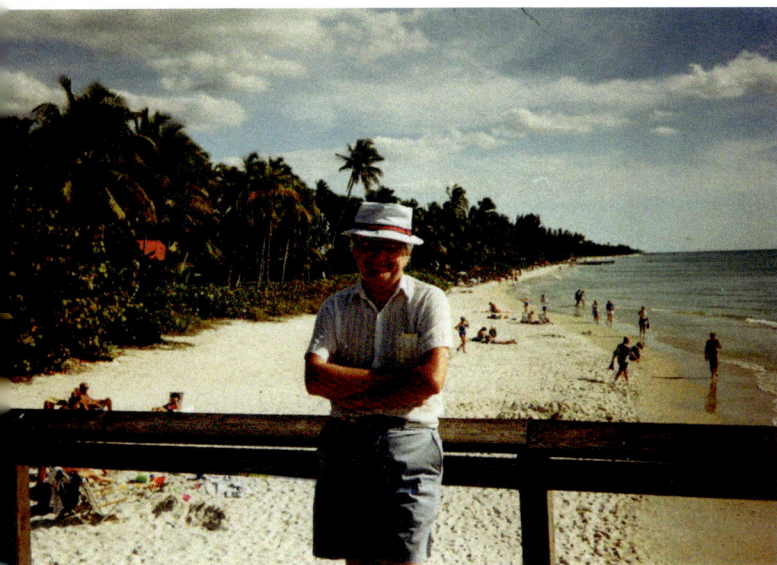

On Naples Pier, Gulf of Mexico 1983

With Pat at an international banquet, Brussels 1978

Entertaining a group of clients and directors at a Wines and Spirits
Benevolent Society dinner at the Park Lane Hotel

Temperature damaged wine invariably loses its colour, aroma and flavour. And, subsequently its value. A brick red-brown colour is an indicator of oxidation damage due to heat. Since sherry is an oxidised wine, another indicator of heat damage in wine is a sherry-like taste.

Where you choose to store your wine should be well ventilated to avoid musty smells, which can penetrate through the cork and affect the quality and flavour of your wine. If keeping your wine at home for any length of time, you should never store it near fruit, vegetables, cheese or anything capable of fermenting.

With these elements that are so difficult to control, it is hardly a surprise that most wines struggle to reach their full potential. And most importantly, less than perfect conditions could put to waste all the consideration and care that has gone into the making of the wine.

THE ESSENTIAL

It is important to store wine at 13-14 degrees Celsius, and to keep that temperature constant for the entire period of its storage.

Wine is like sunshine, held together by water.

Galileo Galilei

Pages from a booklet produced by Octavian about its underground
fine wine storage facility

CHAPTER 6

ONE DOOR CLOSES, ANOTHER OPENS

———⋈———

Careerwise, things for me at Distillers at that time in 1986 would shortly undergo a fundamental change, for my pleasant and secure employment was about to come to an abrupt end. Although Paul was now at university reading law and we were free of the school fees burden we had borne for the past fifteen years, the thought of the loss of such a secure salary was very worrying indeed. It all happened because a man called Ernest Saunders was about to make a big impact on the drinks industry. At the time he was head of Guinness, and right out of the blue they made a bid for Distillers.

As subsequent events proved it was a ridiculous affair, for Guinness was a relatively small company with a market capitalisation around 25% the size of Distillers, which was a highly profitable company and had many very highly valued property assets driving up its asset value. However Saunders was determined to get hold of the brand companies within the group, such as Gordons, Johnnie Walker, Dewars and White Horse, to mention just a few. Many of these brands had highly profitable export markets and were brand leaders.

Saunders borrowed massively and sold off numerous properties to pay back American lenders, and entered into many squalid deals with financiers. Quite remarkable, the city takeover panel just sat on their hands and let it all happen. Eventually it became the largest case of company fraud that had ever hit the City of London, and the outcome was that Saunders and several of his financier friends were put on trial and he and four others were jailed for several years. It was too late to stop the demise of Distillers, and at the age of 51 I was made redundant, along with many others. My employer, the in-house distribution arm of Distillers, was closed down and the distribution function was farmed out to various warehousing and transport companies.

So I was about to become unemployed for the first time in my life and was given a year's redundancy pay. At the time it was difficult at my age to get alternative employment, and indeed some of my management colleagues and directors never worked again. I did have six months' notice of my redundancy, so I started making plans to operate as a self-employed contractor as I felt I was as able as anyone else to, with my years of experience in physical distribution and bonded warehousing, to provide a satisfactory service to Guinness. So I prepared a business plan for my bank in order to raise capital and had meetings with executive within Guinness in an attempt to become a sub-contractor for them in the Midlands and East Anglia which I knew so well.

The idea was similar to a management buyout. I was to take over all the running costs of distribution in return for a five-year contract. Basically it was a cost-plus arrangement I was planning, and I was especially pleased to have the backing of former brand company directors with whom I had been working for nearly twenty years. Also Guinness would have been freed from the stigma of making people unemployed in an area of high unemployment.

However, unknown to me, there were other moves by interested parties going on in the background, and out of the blue I got a phone call from Steve Daniel, the young, thrusting Managing Director of a transport and warehousing company based in the London area, saying he wished to see me the next day, a Friday, at 8 am. He said he had a proposal to put to me face to face and the meeting had to be early because he was travelling up to Manchester for another meeting.

At the meeting Steve told me he knew all about my attempts to secure a management buyout, but his company was also seeking to take on the distribution for Guinness in the Midlands, so it seemed I had become something of a thorn in their side. Without further ado he offered me the job of General Manager Midlands, covering my former activities and two other warehousing sites they had recently acquired there.

He produced a contract of employment, which he had already signed, and said his company, Cert Distribution, was growing rapidly and quietly suggested I should join them rather than get into large financial commitments at my time of life as a self-employed operator. I said I needed the weekend to consider the offer and would let him know on Monday, and then went home to discuss the matter with Pat. When I showed her the job offer, she was over the moon. I knew my redundancy had come as a great shock to her and she had looked at the future with some trepidation, so that evening we went for dinner knowing that I would sign the contract and post it off on Sunday.

So I was back at work without losing a day's pay, in a job with a car and good fringe benefits. You could say I was lucky, but in some ways you make your own luck. In the preceding weeks I had made a number of contacts with the new Guinness company. They had listened to my buy-out proposals, but they had already accepted proposals from Cert Distribution concerning wider issues, and they didn't really want another small contractor to deal with.

A week later, while I was on an induction course at their base in Hoddesdon, I began to realise that working for a small, energetic company would be a world away from working for a blue-chip company like Distillers. At that time Cert's turnover was only £1.5 million, but I was told that through acquisition and organic growth the owner of the company planned to reach £30 million in five years, which would be rapid growth by anyone's standards. The company planned to be the best in drinks distribution but also in high-value goods such as tobacco and perfumes. The capital would come from a venture capitalist in the Channel Isles, and there was plenty of it available for acquisitions. It was a very young company using state of the art IT systems and the latest materials handling techniques, but the thing that struck me most was the young age of the other managers – I was perhaps twenty years older than most of them. The responsibility thrust upon them at such an early age and the enthusiasm and drive they showed were quite electric, and it seemed to me that with such talents this company was really going places. I realised that I would have to move up a gear if I was going to match their pace, but I'd always been a competitor and thought I would be able to match these people; in addition, I had the experience which some of them lacked. In fact within a few months I emerged as a kind of elder statesman, and a few months after that I became the company Transport Director in charge of their fleet operations for the UK, and joined the board with a considerable increase in salary.

It did not require moving, because living in the Midlands was ideal for covering locations in the north and south. By now we had two locations in Scotland, and a good deal of travelling was involved, so I was given a bigger car for comfort. So suddenly, after only 18 months with the company, I was earning much more than I would ever have done with Distillers. It just goes to show that redundancy is not the worst thing that can happen to you, for as one door closes another often opens.

However I had had to change my approach to my working life completely, from a comfortable pedestrian existence to rising at five o'clock each day and working at least a 12-hour day. It was a baptism of fire. I was doing 35,000 miles a year visiting depots across the UK and living out of a suitcase from Monday to Friday, returning to my pattern of life of 30 years earlier.

Cert was entering a period of rapid growth and getting into tobacco, pharmaceuticals and fine wine distribution, but we were tendering for contract warehousing business, where we acquired large sites or built new ones to meet customers' requirements. One such warehouse in the north west accommodated 24,000 pallet positions, stacking the pallets 14 high with fork trucks automated to work under electronic wire guidance. These really were state of the art installations for high-density storage.

I drew on my experience many years before with Dexion, who were world leaders in providing solutions for high-density storage systems. But the company was having growing pains, with little control over personnel recruitment or purchasing, so I left the transport function to take up a new position on the board entitled Resources Director, specifically covering the roles of personnel and buying and purchasing. As a matter of scale, some of these warehouses had over a million pounds' worth of equipment and 100 people, so these functions had to be controlled. We had gone from employing 100 staff to 800 in a couple of years, so the personnel function had to be formalised. Some years earlier I had gained a fair amount of technical assistance from the Institute of Personnel, which covered important aspects such as job specifications, recruitment interviewing, job evaluation and staff appraisal, so I was given the job of developing a personnel policy for this new company and because I'd shown I could get a grip on cost control, all purchasing was put under my control.

Our fleet of vehicles was expanding rapidly. There were over 100 fork trucks across our many depots, including high bay trucks costing over £150,000, and we were buying over 200,000 pallets each year, just to mention a few items. On top of all this, the chairman decided we needed a continental operation, so we acquired a Dutch transport company, based just south of Rotterdam and operating two depots with a fleet of 50 vehicles operating in Holland, Belgium and part of Germany, so this had to be assimilated into Cert's operation system and methods. I had to go across to Holland on several occasions.

On the first trip, I took the Operations Systems Manager with me. Unfortunately he had an aversion to flying. It was only a short flight, from Stansted to Rotterdam, but he insisted on knowing the type of aircraft we would be travelling in and had to be assured that it was a proper jet and not one of the smaller short-haul aircraft. The woman who made our travel arrangements assured him it would be a Boeing, so we had a good trip out, although I could tell he was very nervous.

The day went well and we were able to catch the 6.30 shuttle back. Unfortunately, on arriving at Rotterdam Airport we were told that due to increasingly bad weather over the North Sea our flight would be delayed by an hour or so, so we went to the bar for some drinks. I could see my colleague was getting a little nervous and his normal quite ebullient personality had retreated into its shell. Finally we were called, but unfortunately, because of the disruption, our plane for the return trip would be a Fokker Friendship, a relatively small propeller-driven aircraft. My friend had a tendency to stutter when he was agitated and even more so when he had had a few drinks. He asked the girl on the desk what a F-F-F-F-Fokker Friendship was, and the girl was rather taken aback by his language. I had great difficulty in keeping a straight face.

By the time we were ready for take-off another hour had passed and the wind had virtually reached gale force. Our old plane rumbled down the runway, making a hell of a noise, and my friend was hanging on for dear life. I ordered a couple more large gins, but when the plane finally became airborne it was pitching and tossing all over the place, and we were being sprayed by other people's drinks as they cascaded around the cabin. Eventually the captain told us that he was taking a detour to try to avoid the storm, although this would extend the flight time from 50 minutes to nearly two hours. My colleague was as silent as the grave for the remainder of the flight, and I too was glad to finally get my feet on the ground.

After that we travelled over to Rotterdam quite a few times, always on the overnight car ferry from Harwich to the Hook of Holland, arriving in the office at eight o'clock, before many of our Dutch colleagues.

One colleague, Laurie, became a site director at one of our larger depots. He had an earthy personality and a good sense of humour. On one occasion I visited him and interrogated him about a poor set of monthly management accounts, being concerned about an overrun on his statement for direct labour costs. In his defence he said that sickness, absenteeism and problems of mental health had been adverse factors, and then rather comically went on to blame this on the sex lives of some of his staff. He thought extramarital relations were rife among them, saying 'They're sex mad around here'. He followed this up by saying 'I'd rather have a good shit any time'. This was so unexpected that I nearly fell off my chair with laughter. In fact Laurie was a very bright man.

Cert was now growing at an exciting pace. We had formed a separate company to move into the fine wines storage and distribution business, which we thought might offer better margins than the brand distribution which was our main activity, alongside tobacco and other high-value goods. At this time our MD had responsibility across the whole group and it was decided he should concentrate mainly on core activities, so I was appointed Managing Director of the new company, Octavian Ltd. It had three depots, two in London and a massive underground bonded warehouse at Corsham in Wiltshire. A new start-up company, Octavian was named after the first Roman emperor, which implied that we would be number one in our field. It had been formed only a year earlier and the plan was to consolidate and grow the business organically.

It seemed rather improbable at the time that a run-down, underground, under-utilised, damp and wet storage facility would become within three years the jewel in the crown of the Cert group, but so it turned out. Undoubtedly our chairman, Nigel Jagger, was a visionary. When we had taken it over from Fraser and Company, based in South Wales, it was a derelict former stone quarry masquerading as a bonded warehouse for slow-turnover maturing wines, but our chairman had a vision and a determination to turn it into the best and largest maturation warehouse in the UK, despite its apparent problems. It was a hundred feet below ground and it met all the three requirements for ideal wine storage: there was none of the ultraviolet light which destroys the maturation process, there was no movement to disturb the wine, and it offered a constant temperature. If it was successful, no surface facility would be able to match it.

The place had started life as Gastard Stone Quarry some 200 years earlier and had been worked until the mid-1920s, when demand for Wiltshire stone had apparently been exhausted. The underground workings covered some 30 acres, the equivalent of 14 football pitches. The stone was ideal for building and had been exported all over the world; apparently the municipal buildings in Cape Town are made of Gastard stone. Strangely the stone was quite soft before extraction but it became hard when cut on the surface. There was a million cubic metres still left unmined, should the stone ever become commercially viable again.

Gastard's second life had begun in 1930, when the War Office was looking for strategic storage facilities in the build-up to the Second World War. For the storage of munitions it was considered that a depth of 100 feet was needed to ensure safety from bomb blast. The War Office embarked on a massive project to convert the quarry into an underground store for shells, bombs, torpedoes and anything else which needed protection from possible bomber strikes. At today's prices it would cost several hundred million pounds to convert the honeycomb of underground workings like this. Miles of roadways were constructed, creating an underground village, there was miles of ducting for the air conditioning and massive fans were installed to control the air flow and humidity levels. Lighting and heating had to be provided for the miles of roadways before any ammunition could be stored below. Several inclined planes and lifts had to be constructed to get the goods in and out of the place, indeed several hundred people worked on its construction for several years. Gastard became a key location during the Second World War.

After the war the whole place became derelict and the access points were sealed off. After a caretaking period in the 1940s it was abandoned, until someone came up with the idea that it would be a good place to store wine from the Continent. Unfortunately they had seriously underestimated the work involved and the finance required, and nothing further was done at the time.

Around 1988 I was asked by the main shareholder,

after he had bought the place from the Administrator, to do a quick evaluation of the site and make some initial observations about what it would take to reinstate part of the underground warehouse to create an operational site, along with some idea of the capital outlay required. I had to submit an interim report within a week, typical of the timescales on which Cert operated – most things were demanded yesterday. My first reaction was that this was a bridge too far, even for Cert, where finance was readily available and decisions were made fast. The business we had acquired from Fraser and Company was for low-yielding rental from warehousing and the condition of stock already in storage was very poor and deteriorating, with cases collapsing and bottle labels disintegrating and falling off the bottles, because of the severe damp, even if you could find them in that rambling, poorly-lit place. I could see formidable costs in relabelling foreign-bottled stocks and endless repacking costs when stock had to be withdrawn at point of sale. The cost of claims for lost or damaged stock was also likely to be considerable.

It was ironic that although the state of the bottle labels and cases was very poor, the condition of the wine inside was excellent. Our clients were constantly complaining about the condition of their stock when it was presented for sale, and the site was not well regarded in the trade. Continental underground warehouses also had problems with damp, but most wine over there was stored horizontally in racks and only labelled and cased when it was needed for shipment, so it could arrive in pristine condition.

In 1988, when I first visited the site, it was like driving onto a disused airfield. Four hundred yards from the main road there were a few Portakabins, but there were no other site buildings, just a small enclosure protecting the winch which hauled small bogie trucks up and down the inclined plane to the goods-received department a hundred feet below ground. There was no means of access for personnel other than a single flight of 300 steps, just a yard wide, so they went up and down them all the time as a matter of course, because under the Mining and Quarries Act it was forbidden to ride the winch bogies. People worked underground every day and it seemed to me that we would have difficulties retaining staff in this somewhat strange working environment. Only about ten per cent of the underground area was in use and the electricity installations were very old and somewhat dangerous. I considered it would be costly to rewire the present area and electrify additional areas to increase storage capacity.

I remember on my first visit being shown around the area we were using and then taken down into the unused area, walking perhaps half a mile into the dark areas equipped only with a flashlight and a voice recorder and wearing wellingtons and heavy duffel coat to keep warm. I smelled an all-consuming dampness which seemed to remain on my clothes for days. It was a most eerie place to be. I suppose my advice was to cut and run from a facility which was obviously going to be a continuous drain on finance – literally a black hole. To spend a couple of million pounds on such a high-risk venture seemed highly questionable.

Corsham's previous reputation among the trade under the management of Fraser and Company was not good. At that time there were only 50,000 cases in store and we were of the opinion that we would have to increase its capacity to something like 500,000, which would mean going into the wettest part of the workings, where humidity levels were much higher and there was no lighting, so considerable capital expenditure would be required. But the shareholders had large pockets and were determined to make Corsham the biggest underground bonded storage warehouse in Europe. Wine sales were increasing rapidly, so servicing this activity placed us in a growth industry.

As Managing Director of Octavian I was based at Charlton, where we had a large bonded warehouse previously managed by a large Spanish sherry importer, but we turned it into our principal hub looking after the London and South East trade, which at the time was perhaps 70 per cent of the UK market, and I then had a board of four looking after the usual management functions. From the outset we focused on selling our Corsham operation with very bold advertising and marketing, extolling the virtues of holding stock in an underground maturation warehouse, and we picked up thousands of private clients who bought fine wine for investment purposes, ex-cellars in France and elsewhere. We also took the opportunity to speak to principal wine importers with a view to having their fine wines placed in a cellarage operation rather than having vintage wines stored in surface warehouses in the south east, where these high-value wines virtually baked in the summer and froze in the winter. We knew these other warehouse keepers did not offer the correct solution for maturing wines.

There was quite an amusing episode in the early days when Octavian Limited was first set up as a company. For a year while permanent offices were being constructed, we took a small suite of offices to house four directors and a couple of office staff. We choose to take a few offices on the ground floor, so we virtually looked straight out on the street from our windows, but it was a matter of any port in a storm – just temporary

I remember it was summertime and we had the sash windows open to create reasonable ventilation. At the end of the working day, as is the custom in London, the four of us usually went for a drink, and three of us had put on our jackets ready to depart. However the finance director couldn't find his jacket and he accused Jeremy, our sales director, who was a jovial character, of fooling around and hiding it. He clearly remembered hanging the jacket over the back of his chair next to the open window, but it was not to be found. He never did get his jacket back. We worked out that someone on the pavement outside, using a stick or similar implement, must have lifted it from the chair back, skilfully withdrawn it through the open window and made off with jacket and contents.

So we sat in the pub, Mark jacketless. I must have a strange sense of humour, as I couldn't help feeling amused by the whole incident – its execution was so audacious.

When we had finished our drinks and went outside to the car park, I was still sniggering a little. But Steve, my fellow director, had seen something which would quickly take the smile off my face. He told me to take a look at my BMW. Someone had thrown bricks through the windscreen and side windows and stolen the radio and

CD player and a coat, among other things. There was broken glass everywhere, and the car was not driveable. I had to spend the next two hours arranging and waiting for a breakdown truck and a loan car.

We had open days at Corsham, and drinks trade magazines such as *Decanter* were invited to visit the site, all in the hope of getting good trade publicity. Meanwhile things were happening. We built a small surface warehouse to accommodate goods received and goods forwarding operations and a new winching mechanism was installed to enable speedier movement of pallets into and out of the underground warehouse.

Down below we built an office complex with visiting and tasting facilities, furnished and carpeted to the most luxurious standards. The idea was to present an image of a quality operation. I personally acquired racking for thousands of pallet positions to better utilise space and also get produce off the damp passageways. It gave the place some order and was essential for stock control to the central computer. We spent heavily on humidity control, with sensors placed throughout the twenty-five acres of underground chambers and walkways, and we invested in many mobile dehumidifiers which could be moved to areas most in need. I got used to fortnightly visits there to walk the gangways, smell the dampness in particular areas and feel the condition of the Fiberite cases, which were at risk from the high humidity levels. The timely movement of a machine could prevent stock being damaged and remove gallons of water from the atmosphere to be pumped away. If we hadn't done that we would have been left with a lot of re-casing to do.

It took us well over a year to conquer the humidity problem, largely working by trial and error. We expected adding volume to the storage capacity to reduce the areas of high humidity, but this principle was challenged by our air-conditioning specialists. We came to understand that autumn was the most difficult period to get through – the dew point was significant to the difference between underground and surface humidity levels, and this increased at certain times of the year, but the key to controlling humidity was more monitoring and electronic control.

After much experimentation, we took the facility to a point where Corsham was recognised as perhaps the best warehouse in the UK for keeping fine wine for long periods. The need to continue volume storage was the key, not fast turnover, and high-value investors were the target. So the need was to develop the higher end of the storage market, and we agreed to appoint a sales executive as a 'door opener' focusing on high-end financial investors.

As a well-known player in this market I had a constant flow of CVs coming across my desk. One day Nigel Jagger, our chairman, received a CV which particularly impressed him, and he told me to get the applicant in and have a look at him.

Oliver Shepard was an old Etonian who had spent several years after school as a Guards officer, followed by some years in management in the brewing industry, so he knew the drinks trade. I had had years of interviewing all kinds of people and I had learned to regard the first half-minute of an interview as very important – the first impressions syndrome – thanks to my training under Bill Isbister twenty years before.

Oliver was totally confident as he walked towards my desk wearing a ready smile, clean- shaven, not a hair out of place and impeccably dressed with shining shoes. Quite frankly, I had to give him ten out of ten. He didn't sit down until he was invited to do so, didn't attempt to move the chair, and then remained silent. What an entrance! I have to say that I have never liked interviewing from CVs – they tend to be manufactured, with plenty of gaps to hide career indiscretions or shortcomings. For a moment it appeared so with Oliver, whose CV indicated that he had not been gainfully employed for the past couple of years. This looked rather fishy, so I asked him what he had been up to. His explanation was rather fascinating. Apparently an old school pal from Eton, Ranulph Fiennes (later to become famous as Sir Ranulph), had put together a team to go on a Transglobe Overland Expedition. Their small group had to be very fit, good skiers and good marksmen, and each had to be able to carry out a specific job for the team. Oliver had been nominated as medical man for the group as well as their 'tooth merchant'. Fiennes was well known in royal circles and I believe Prince Charles was patron to the expedition. So Oliver became accustomed to visiting Clarence House, the home of the Queen Mother. This was what Oliver had been doing for the past two or three years; he clearly knew his way around high society.

Nigel and I compared notes and we offered him a job as Sales Executive. We thought his knowledge of the hotel and restaurant business in the West End would make him a very good 'door opener', as he seemed to be on first-name terms with a lot of people in high office.

Oliver made one request of me when we signed an employment contract, which was that I should allow him to be absent one afternoon each month. Apparently over recent years he had formed a friendship with the Queen Mother and Prince Charles and would take afternoon tea at Clarence House with them monthly. How could I refuse such a request? He was a really nice guy to have around, and being a former Guards officer he knew the chain of command.

I lost touch with Oliver on retirement, but some years later I heard he held a position at Purdeys, the luxury gunmaker in Mayfair. Once again he was at the top end of the market.

To continue, volume storage was the key, not fast turnover. We had to show potential clients that the tide had changed at Corsham, and as a publicity initiative I was instructed to buy a silver salver from Aspreys to present to the client storing the millionth case at Corsham since its rehabilitation. This was duly presented to the winners, the wine importer Percy Fox & Co.

In a high-value storage business, security is usually a matter of prime concern. At Corsham, however, because it was mainly below ground, security was not a problem. However, there was still a threat from unscrupulous elements within the trade. Around that time certain wine merchants were converting stock they had bought on behalf of private investment clients into their own stock balances and ultimately selling it. The first time a private client would discover this fraudulent activity was when he called on the warehouse keeper to sell and found there was no stock. The Greens case in London was the first incident, when hundreds of private clients were robbed of their stock by this particular wine company. This practice was stamped out, and Octavian was at the forefront in devising physical stock control methods which highlighted the fact that private clients had title ownership of their stock and each case was so marked so that it could not be converted into an importer's bulk stockholdings.

Our terms of trade were set up to inspire confidence among high-value private investors, and we focused on these procedures in our drive to attract the growing private market, inviting these clients to visit Corsham from time to time to inspect their stock during the maturation process, which might have taken place over several years.

At surface warehouses such as our main centre in London, security was a daily ongoing problem, and we had responsibility for several top brands. Octavian had up to 20 vans at Charlton operating within the Greater London area, but dedicated villains operated independently pursuing their own audacious crimes.

Although we were the largest bonded warehouse company in the London area we had to keep a constant watch on the competition, which was out to capture our wine importing business. I experienced a strange development after the break-up of the Soviet Union and its Eastern European satellites in 1989. This concerned a former state-owned company in Bulgaria, Bulgarian Vintners Ltd, to which we had been supplying warehousing facilities for a number of years. We had got used to their Christmas trade and were making provisional plans to accept their usual trade, which was in the order of 300,000 cases a year.

My sales manager, who was chasing the business, was informed that after the communist government in Sofia had collapsed, Bulgarian Vintners had also folded, and the red wine label BVL no longer existed. Then right out of the blue, the chap who had been BVL's managing director rang us from a small office in the Limehouse area of London and told us he was now trading as a new company. To cut a long story short, he and another enterprising chap had seized the opportunity when the nationalised company had collapsed to continue trading under the name Domain Boyar, and they were already selling the brand to Tesco and other supermarkets. His phone call was to tell us that several containers were on the way to our bonded warehouse, and to say he trusted that trade terms would remain the same as for the former company. This kind of take-over of businesses happened all the time in Eastern Europe after communism collapsed, and the former state managers suddenly became very enterprising – and of course very rich – when these sudden business opportunities came their way because they were in the right place at the right time. They paid their bills, and it was for others to make judgments. The Domain Boyar label still exists.

On the career front, I had by now been with the Cert Group for four years and I had achieved much more than I had ever imagined possible when I was made redundant in 1986. But then quite suddenly the group managing director decided to head for pastures new and I was asked to take on his role with a much-enhanced salary, leaving my post as MD of Octavian but remaining with the firm as a director. This meant a return to the Cert head office at Hoddesdon, from which I controlled the operations of both companies. Group turnover was now about £35m with a total payroll of about 800 people spread across ten operating centres, and that meant a good deal of travelling, mostly by car, covering some 35,000 miles a year. I was living out of a suitcase in the week and returning to Claverley most weekends. The job was all-consuming, and a depot like Warrington, which was a hub for our brand goods distribution, needed my constant attention. Our largest customer, United Distillers, pushed six million cases a year through the depot annually, and like all our other depots it was a 24-hour operation.

Around this time, completely out of the blue, I had

two confrontations with gypsies. I had never had any experience of dealing with gypsies, or travellers, as they prefer to be called, but during 1990 I was deeply involved with two incidents involving them. On each occasion, without any warning, they simply descended onto our premises and their occupation had dire consequences for our business and the locality.

The first happened when, one Monday morning, I was suddenly confronted with the news that fifty or so caravans had during the early hours moved on to our lorry park in Charlton, South London, while it was empty over the weekend. The police had already been informed that this was private property and signs were displayed to that effect, but they refused to help us in any way. We operated about fifty vehicles, and trailers from the site and overnight arrivals were already queueing on the streets (and this was an urban area), blocking local residents' driveways and our own employees, perhaps 150 or so, could not park anywhere when they arrived for work, and a flock of policemen were threatening anyone who tried to park in their own streets. One senior police officer even suggested I should close the depot while he tried to sort things out.

The gypsies had caused a scene of utter chaos and we had hundreds of customers waiting for their 'just in time' deliveries. The only people who were pressing on normally were the gypsies and their followers in their big Mercedes and Range Rovers – perhaps two hundred of them.

During the day I watched them coming off and onto the site doing their normal business, selling their merchandise to the local householders or those in the scrap business, bringing all kinds of scrap by the ton to be sorted in our car park, which now looked like a dumping ground. There was only one entrance and it was surrounded by an eight-foot chain-link fence. As a matter of interest, each local authority in an urban area usually has a Traveller Liaison Officer, and ours attended the depot. We hoped he would bring his expertise in such matters to the fore and secure a swift resolution, but rather like the police, his sympathies were very much with the travellers, and he was almost suggesting that the truck park was like a 'haven of rest' for these poor harmless people in their £50,000 travelling caravans. So I quickly realised that that this had to be a matter of self-help, otherwise these travellers would stay on our private property, driving on and off at will and cocking a snook at the company, the police and the local householders.

This state of affairs went on for a few days, and our business was being badly disrupted. I began to conceive a plan to wrest back control from these scallywags. Most mornings by about nine o'clock all their cars and vans had left the site to do whatever to go about their business, so I said to the police inspector that I had a plan in place to stop them coming back onto the site in the evening with their ill-gotten gains and scattering them in our park. The principal element of this was to block their re-entry with a 14-metre trailer. The inspector was not keen, but by this time he was seeking any solution, and he agreed to my request to provide 24-hour protection to prevent criminal damage to our trailers parked in the entrance.

That afternoon when the gypsies returned and saw their way blocked, all hell was let loose. Further police arrived and the liaison officer returned, but he quickly went away again after speaking to the gypsy leader. I think he realised that the end game was not far away.

The streets were lined with local residents who knew that now a real confrontation was about to take place. The police told the gypsies that they could not park their vehicles in the side streets, and they were instructed to put their vans in a public park a quarter of a mile away. Our car park ceased to be used as a trading post, so we had cut off their lifeblood, so to speak.

The following morning a peace plan was agreed whereby the police agreed that one by one the travellers' cars would be allowed back on the site to connect up their caravans. They did so and by lunchtime all were gone, leaving our site in a filthy condition with dog and human excrement all over the place and piles of rubbish everywhere. It took nearly a whole day to get our truck park back into use.

But that wasn't the end of the gypsies. Just a few months later at a large depot used as a hub trunking depot between England and Scotland, located at Warrington, again early one Monday morning, I was told that in the early hours of Saturday or Sunday a large group of caravans, approximately 150, and over 500 people had suddenly encamped on our trailer park. This incident was a much more serious problem in terms of numbers and potential financial implications, and two of our large clients, Bells and Gordons, were likely to be affected.

Once again the police were immediately involved and once again the Traveller Liaison Officer from the local authority was notified. But this time I knew the way forward. I told the Chief Inspector what I intended doing on the Monday afternoon, but I did not disclose my plans to the Traveller Liaison Officer, because once again his sympathies were with the travellers, who had come from as far afield as the Midlands with their fancy caravans to occupy our privately-owned three-acre lorry park. The volume here was much greater. We operated 50 wagons from this site and in addition more than forty 14-metre trailers carrying over 30,000 cases of gin and whisky came through the depot daily.

I explained to the Chief Inspector what I planned to do. When the gypsies had departed to go about their business on the Tuesday morning, I would once again block the entrance to the trailer park with a 14-metre trailer, preventing them from getting their vehicles back in. But the Chief Inspector was not happy. With so many travellers and their families involved, he feared it would cause a serious breach of the peace, as he put it. To this I replied that my clients were foremost in my mind and the incident would be in private land and would not affect the public. Furthermore I would hire private security men with guard dogs if necessary to protect our vehicles. I simply said that I thought it was his responsibility to protect the peace.

Eventually he agreed to police the situation on the Tuesday afternoon. Again all hell was let loose when the travellers' vehicles were not allowed to join their caravans and families, but eventually, as at Charlton, they were allowed in one by one to collect their caravans and move on, and this they did. The incident was all over in a matter of days, and the tactics we had developed at

Charlton were as successful here.

Travellers lead a strange way of life, but they are quite ruthless, and some of them can be very dangerous people indeed.

At weekends at this time I had only Saturday and part of Sunday free, because by lunchtime on Sunday I was preparing for the next week on the road. I was mainly travelling south, and in times of bad weather I would travel down late on Sunday to a plush Thamesside flat the company provided in London, or rise early on Monday morning to ensure I was in the office at Hoddesdon before 8.30. I quite enjoyed the pressure and the tension, and I suppose at that time a twelve-hour day was quite normal, but companies do not grow rapidly without special effort.

I was very fortunate throughout my working life never to have a mundane job or experience what is known as 'that Monday morning feeling'. I always enjoyed my work and never felt unable to perform my duties, and it continued to be so in my last role as Group Managing Director.

On reflection, I felt the least enjoyable time was when I had to deal with the trade unions in those crazy years of the 1970s and 80s when industrial unrest was always simmering. Split loyalties between workforce and management were very much the order of the day, and politics was invading the workplace all the time. I was somewhat fortunate that when I was eventually responsible for a large workforce, union shop-floor power had been set aside by Parliamentary legislation and within Cert Distribution, only in Scotland did we have a large number of card-carrying union members.

However, the unions had not gone away just yet. At Hoddesdon one day I received a letter from the District Secretary of the Transport and General Workers' Union suggesting that the majority of Cert workers at its many depots were members of the union and they wanted union rights to recognition and the appointment of shop stewards for joint consultation and wage bargaining rights. The shareholders were not at all happy with this turn of events. I was sceptical of the union's claims and set out on the quiet to find out from the depot managers and directors what the state of play was, giving them 14 days to elicit the true picture confidentially. In the meantime I avoided the T&G's request for a face-to-face meeting, as I did not want to give them the idea that there was any hint of recognition.

Eventually the collated figures showed that at only one Scottish depot was there any show of membership, and even there it was not a majority. At most depots a few employees were members, but no more. So it was with a good deal of satisfaction that my Operations Director and I agreed to meet the TGWU London District Secretary and his assistant at a neutral hotel location, as I was certainly not going to give him any hint of success. It gave me great pleasure to pass on this information, along with a very clear indication that Cert plc would not be recognising his union. This was clearly an attempt by the TGWU to gain control. Remembering the bad old days when a driver could not make a delivery to the customer without a union card, and all the closed-shop activities of the union, we and the shareholders were glad to be out of the grip of the union. We never heard from them again, but then we always paid our workforce above union rates to keep them away.

My time as Managing Director was largely focused on analysing monthly feedback statistic and management accounts for the ten operating centres, questioning general managers on their throughput and performance and seeing client managers from our principal customers. Positive cash flow was at the heart of the business, and bearing in mind that we had over three thousand clients we needed an army of credit controllers to get money banked at a time in the early 90s when for several years the bank rate was over 10 per cent. Some of our largest customers were the worst offenders in taking extra days of credit, so a good credit controller was worth their weight in gold. Positive cashflow is the lifeblood of any business, and at this time my early training in accountancy thirty years before was useful in meeting the demands of higher business control.

A fair amount of my time was taken up in preparing for monthly meetings of the two companies. The main shareholder would always fly in from abroad to attend, and sometimes immediately afterwards a meeting would be held to make a presentation to an anticipated new client. I remember one such occasion when we were to have an afternoon meeting with Wella, the big German cosmetics company. Knowing the Germans' disciplined approach to such meetings, I had briefed the directors who would be making presentations to wear smart blue or grey business suits and white or blue shirts, certainly not brown shoes or red ties, and if necessary to get their hair trimmed. I was considerably older that the other four who would be making presentations, so as the only grey-haired guy around I declined to attend. We wanted to present a company run by energetic young executives.

The shareholder who was to give the presentation on the company's financial background rarely wore a suit and usually wore his hair shoulder length. I felt this could present a problem, so I suggested that on this occasion he might like to attend wearing a sober lounge suit and perhaps a light hair trim might be appropriate. Fortunately he agreed to go along with this. When we met up for the pre-meeting discussion he turned up in a very well-tailored grey double-breasted suit and thanked me for persuading him to wear it, as he had not worn it for some years. He then surprised himself by producing from the inside pocket a large brown envelope containing several thousand pounds. I had never before met anyone who could have left so much money hanging in a wardrobe for so long without realising it, but he was a rich man.

One of his hobbies was collecting valuable motor cars, holding them for a few years while they appreciated in value and selling them on. He seemed to have a collection of 20 or so of these. On one occasion we had a company weekend at Brocket Hall, one of the reasons for this choice being that we were to have a private viewing of Lord Brocket's famous car collection. The most interesting of these was an American Cord, a wine and cream-coloured two-seater convertible circa 1950, formerly owned by Aly Khan, the socialite and racehorse owner who was married to the Hollywood actress Rita Hayworth in the 1950s. That was the first car I ever saw with a phone. How unfortunate that a few years later Lord Brocket destroyed his multi-million pound collection as part of an insurance scam for which he went to prison. At the time when I met him and Lady Brocket they seemed a charming couple, perhaps in their mid-thirties. In truth all cannot have been well at Brocket Hall.

Around the time of the Brocket scandal, a massively controversial affair which affected our company occurred in the City of London. To me the timescale of this affair spanned more than thirty years, and the main participants had featured in different aspects of my life over this extended period.

It's a long story and one which had started years before when I was an impecunious railway clerk in Northwich. At that time one of my colleagues on the shipping desk was a fellow called Bob Gunn, who was perhaps fifteen years older than me. He was a bright guy and a very keen sportsman who kept wicket for Northwich Cricket Club. He had a young son, John, who was equally good at cricket and a good batsman, opening the batting for his school, Sir John Deane's Grammar School in Northwich – Pat attended the school at the same time. I found John a quiet and studious lad. The Gunn family were well known to us. They lived in a council house about half a mile from my home at Bleak House Farm. They didn't own a car and both parents were out at work each day, Mrs Gunn at a milliner's shop in Northwich.

John was a bright lad with a penchant for languages, and he went on to gain a degree in modern languages at Nottingham University before joining Barclays Bank at the local branch. But he was destined for greater things. He was transferred to the bank's head office to use his language skills in the foreign currency department in Manchester. At this stage he was clearly a man with a mission, and he did a postgraduate course at a German university and some time afterwards married a German girl. He and his new wife returned to Cheshire and lived in a semi-detached house near our farm; my father delivered their milk daily.

Then quite suddenly they were gone, and it wasn't until some years later that I heard of John again. I read in the *Financial Times* that he had been head-hunted by a Singapore organisation which was in the money-dealing business, to head up a new company. From the figures quoted it appeared he was going to make a lot of money. The article seemed to suggest that he had become of the smartest foreign currency experts in the financial world, and his name was frequently quoted as a top man in his field.

Meanwhile a young man called John Fulston had dreamed up a marketing scheme involving the lease of computer hardware, and he launched a company in London called Atlantic Computers. He turned to a venture capitalist, someone I knew something about, to raise money for the proposed venture. Len Jagger, a Jersey-based businessman and backer of bright ideas, loaned him several million to get his show on the road in return for the usual equity stake. With Fulston's drive Atlantic Computers grew very quickly to become one of the biggest leasing companies in the world.

Unfortunately Fulston had a liking for fast cars, and while driving a racing car at Silverstone he had a fatal accident. Atlantic was a not a one-man band, but John Fulston had been its driving force, so suddenly the company appeared to be up for grabs.

Who should now appear on the scene but John Gunn, who had made a remarkable move up in the financial world and was now boss of the British and Commonwealth Banking Company, one of the most prestigious investment banks in London and the Far East. On behalf of B&C he made a bid of a few hundred million pounds for the control of Atlantic Computers – a big deal by any standards. To secure the deal he had to persuade our venture capitalist, who by now was a principal shareholder, to sell his shares. Eventually a deal was done and Atlantic was now owned by British and Commonwealth and chaired by John Gunn.

But things began to unravel quickly. In fact Atlantic

had been vastly overvalued, and the result was one of the biggest fraud investigations in the history of the City of London. British and Commonwealth, which had large borrowings, began to crumble under the pressure of the scandal, and unfortunately for the shareholders it went bust. This was headline news in the *Times* and *Telegraph* for weeks.

Financial scandals happen when money simply disappears. For several months financial journalists and reporters and cameramen were all over the place looking for leads, and it didn't take much probing to find out that Cert plc was largely owned by the same group of venture capitalists from Jersey, so for some weeks I had packs of reporters outside our head office, seeking information for their columns. I gave instructions that no interviews were to be given, and our security guards did a good job; none of the press were allowed past the gatehouse and onto the site.

So that was the rise and fall of John Gunn over the thirty years I was acquainted with his family. He naturally lost his job, as British and Commonwealth no longer existed. However you cannot keep a good man down, and after some years in the doldrums I hear John is back in the city and doing well again. The Jagger family also continue to prosper and still live in Jersey, although

Len Jagger died some years ago. I believe the Fulstons still have some interest in racing, but now live abroad. Business is of course about taking risks, and I don't regard such people as scallywags.

Although I still enjoyed my work, I had by now achieved far more than my personal career objectives and felt that I had no further goals to pursue. I was now approaching 60 and still handling the workload of a 40-year-old.

One Friday night I was returning home for the weekend down the M1. I always delayed my journey home until the early evening to avoid the usual Friday-night build up at the southern end of the M1. At about half past seven I was passing through the Luton area and cruising along in my BMW at my usual 75 mph and looking forward to getting home in about two hours, which would allow time to go to one of the local pubs for dinner with Pat. It was raining steadily and darkness was falling. Suddenly and without warning, the engine cut out. The power steering, brakes and lighting all lost power and the car started to lose speed. I quickly realised I needed to get from the fast lane to the hard shoulder, but the middle lane was full of heavy goods vehicles thundering past. I put on my hazard lights and after a few moments, with some difficulty, I managed to thread my way onto the hard shoulder, where I sat for a couple of minutes attempting to recover and working out what to do next. I was very conscious of the vehicles roaring past to my right a few feet away and realised that the hard shoulder was not the place to be, so after making a call to the breakdown recovery service I grabbed my raincoat and got out of the car. By now it was raining heavily, so I scrambled over the motorway boundary into a field to await the arrival of the recovery vehicle.

After an hour or so the vehicle turned up, and after some delay because of the darkness the car was eventually winched aboard the truck. By now we were both completely drenched. The driver told me he would be taking me to Leighton Buzzard, about 20 miles away. When we got there it was after 9 pm and I was told nothing could be done at that hour and nobody in the garage understood the sophisticated electronics of the BMW. The nearest dealer was at Luton, and they were of course closed for the night. I did think about staying there overnight, but there was no guarantee that the car would be fixed the following morning; it showed no signs of life at all. There were no hire cars available and public transport to Shropshire was non-existent, so a taxi was the only way of getting home, but this was Friday night, very busy for the taxi trade, and a ride of 100 miles with no return fare was not good business for them. However I managed to get a driver to take me home on the basis that I would pay him for the return journey as well.

We set off heading north, but he refused to go via the motorway system and had no idea where Shropshire even was, so I plotted a route for him using good classified A roads via Coventry and Birmingham to my home at Claverley. When we finally got there just after two o'clock on Saturday morning I was still wet through to my underpants. Both my mobile and the driver's were out of charge and I had not been able to make contact with home for three hours. When I finally entered the house I was a sorry sight for Pat to behold, but I reflected how lucky I had been not to have been involved in a serious accident.

Some years before this I was involved in a motorway pile-up on the M1 just north of Newport Pagnell. I was travelling south at about 80mph in the outside lane when I noticed a Vauxhall Cavalier indicating to leave the motorway. As he approached the slip road his speed reduced to a crawl, and as a result a heavy goods vehicle behind him in the same lane hit him and knocked the Cavalier right across the motorway into my lane. I lost sight of him for a few seconds, but then I saw the car hit the central barrier and spin round, and suddenly it was coming towards me in the fast lane. The result was chaos across all three lanes with vehicles crashing into each other, and I was very aware of 40-tonne articulated vehicles very close to my nearside. My instant concern was what to do about the Cavalier that was flying towards me. Fortunately I was in a big car fitted with ABS and I was able to brake in a straight line. I hit him head on, but by the time of the impact my speed was down to only 15mph or so, although I dented his front end somewhat. There was still mayhem going on all round, but all I felt was a slight nudge from behind.

After a short while the whole motorway came to a grinding halt. Eventually the police arrived, and after about half an hour they had managed to clear a path to allow vehicles that had not been involved in the pile-up to get through. They looked at my car and separated me from the Cavalier, whose driver had said to me a few minutes earlier that he had thought his number was up when he saw me rushing towards him. Then with the aid of crowbars the police managed to prise my bumper bar away from the tyres. They then instructed me to start the car and test the steering. When they were satisfied it was OK to drive, they asked me where I was going and told me to get on my way but to drive slowly, both for my benefit and the car's.

An hour later I arrived at the garage which was to repair the car and hired a replacement. I mentioned the incident to Sadie, my secretary, but told her to keep quiet about it. When I arrived home the following Friday Pat asked why I was driving a different car and I told her mine was in for service. I did not tell her about the pile-up until a few years later, when I had retired. I decided at the time that there was no point in worrying her.

The breakdown incident on the M1 was the turning point in my decision to retire. I was conscious that on several occasions during late evening drives home to Shropshire I had felt extreme tiredness whilst driving and could have been in danger of falling asleep at the wheel, so a fortnight after the breakdown I decide to give a year's notice of my decision to pack up work at the age of 60. The Chairman was surprised at my decision because we had never previously talked about it, and he considered it would take nine months to recruit and train a successor and hand over my responsibilities. Fortunately, during my final three months I was able to reduce my hours to three days a week.

The new Managing Director, a chartered accountant and former finance director of a large electrical distributor, quickly got up to speed and I spent most of my final months on a large project in Scotland. The company had just secured a large contract with United Distillers to handle the containerisation and forwarding activities of a large part of their export trade to the United States, some six million cases per year, and the contract was for five years with an option beyond. This would be a stand-alone operation from our operations in Scotland. The only problem was that we did not have a suitable warehouse in Scotland to deal with the business, but we had 22 weeks to get the job ready for the export drive which essentially got under way in September ready for the American Christmas trading season.

So we were looking for a big shed or warehouse of 200,000 square feet with at least 7 metres to the eaves, located in the broad belt of industrial Scotland near Glasgow, and estate agents were briefed with our requirements. At the time Scotland was going through a recession and there were many empty industrial buildings, often in derelict condition, on Clydeside.

I tramped around the area for a couple of weeks looking around the former car plant at Linwood and a large former Rolls Royce factory abandoned several years earlier, and it was a dismal scene. It seemed the Scots were not cut out to make motor cars, as the abandoned British Leyland plant at Bathgate was also nearby. Fortunately for us at least, the steel industry was also in recession and we were offered an empty steel stockholding warehouse some 15 miles east of Glasgow with excellent access to the Scottish motorway network, another factor which we had listed as essential, as we wanted to ensure that our many heavy goods vehicles would not have to travel through urban areas. The site was also well positioned to receive large movements from the Scottish bottling plants as we expected it would be handling 30,000 cases per day.

So we negotiated to take over this 10-acre site, built about 20 years before with a single warehouse with plenty of office and messing facilities surrounded by a 2-metre high perimeter fence. However, having been a custom-built steel stocking warehouse, it had no concrete floor. Steel warehouses just pyramid their 25-ton steel reels and they sit on earth, as no ordinary concrete floor would be able to deal with the weights involved. It was just a big shed and not really a warehouse. We knew we would have to floor the place, and our conversion budget of £300,000 included this work. To satisfy the Customs & Excise fire requirements we would have to sectionalise the building into half a dozen smaller areas. We would also have to install 20ft fire doors to minimise the fire risk in this bonded whisky warehouse. At one end of the building we had to install many dock levellers so that we could deal with arrivals and despatches simultaneously. So there was plenty of work to be done, not least 25,000 building blocks to construct the sectional walls. I appointed a main contractor who we had used before to build warehouses in the Yorkshire area, as they were used to doing much larger contracts for us and to building to a tight time scale.

I travelled up to Scotland at least once a week, always on a Friday, and as I was in charge of the project, every Friday at 11 am I called a progress meeting on site at which all contractors would be present, ostensibly to ensure we were in line with our time scales, and progress would be chased if there were any delays.

All went well for the first two weeks, but then a strike at the factory supplying us with building blocks brought progress to a halt. Top Bloc, a subsidiary of the Tarmac Group, who were based at Wolverhampton, gave no indication to our main contractor when supplies would be commenced again, so I spoke directly to the managing director to tell him of the urgency involved and informing him of our intention to break contract and get supplies elsewhere, but it was two weeks before blocks started arriving on site again, and by the end of week seven we were nearly three weeks behind schedule. However blocks were now arriving on site at the rate of

1000 a day, so the bricklayers, who had been idle for three weeks, had plenty of stock available, so I travelled up for the customary Friday progress meeting for week seven knowing there was some rescheduling needed to get back on track.

On inspecting the site with the site manager before going into the meeting I was surprised to find no bricklayers there, and on asking why I was told that Scottish bricklayers did not work on Friday afternoons. This frustrated me somewhat and I realised it would have to be dealt with. At the meeting, I asked for the bricklayers' gangmaster to plan for the following week's overtime to be worked on Friday afternoon and Saturday and the same for the following two weeks, saying I was determined to get the project back on target. I was amazed when he told me that there was no chance they would do as I requested, repeating that his men did not work on Friday afternoons. I pointed out to him that our contract stipulated that overtime working was part of their contractual obligations, but he would not change his position. When I suggested he should take on more men, he said he could not get them at such short notice.

I adjourned the meeting for two hours and quickly got into private discussion with the Leeds-based site manager with a view to getting 30 bricklayers from the Yorkshire and Lancashire areas, men who had worked for us on building projects in North West England. While the site manager was rounding up prospective bricklayers I was planning to get a number of Portakabins and extra security on site for Sunday, and I was soon pleased to hear from the site manager that he had been successful in his mission, following his assurance that they would be well remunerated.

We reconvened after lunch and I asked the gangmaster if he had reconsidered his decision and he speedily replied that he had not. I then told him he had therefore broken the written contractual obligations and we were accordingly dispensing with him and his bricklayers and we would not be requiring them on Monday morning. I also told him there would be extra security and the police would be informed in case there were any difficulties. He was astounded, to say the least, and asked how the brickwork would be dealt with. I simply said that the job would be completed, and he left the meeting abruptly, very angry, while I continued to deal with the other sub-contractors.

The English bricklayers travelled up to Scotland on the Sunday afternoon and were housed in the Portakabins, fed and watered and told not to leave the site. I also asked the site agent to remain on the site over the weekend and arrange for the bricklaying to start at 7.30 on Monday morning. There was a certain amount of huffing and puffing at the start of work on the Monday morning, but the Scottish bricklayers were not admitted to the site and the main gate was kept closed. Happily enough the whole of the brickwork was completed four weeks later and we were back on target and ready for the other finishing trades to get on with their work programmes. They too completed their work on time, after which the main contractor handed over the site for us to begin a programme of recruitment and training for a workforce of 60 or so people.

That was really the last challenge in my working career, one where grit, determination and judgment were the characteristics needed to get through a challenging set of circumstances. I doubt if I would have got away with this in the 1970s when the unions and the shop floor ruled much of British industry, and Scotland had always been a hotbed of militancy.

CHAPTER 7

FINAL YEARS WITH PAT

—◦◦◦◦◦—

So to retirement. Because I had been such a workaholic over the years, many people thought I would have great difficult when it came to retiring, and it may be true that in the New Year of 1995 I approached it with some trepidation. However, Pat and immediately I set off in the car to the Continent to spend an extended period in Spain. We got the ferry across the Bay o0f Biscay from Portsmouth to Bilbao and drove via Madrid to the town of Estepona, where an acquaintance of ours had a seaside villa.

Lo and behold, after a stay of ten weeks away from the daily round and the usual tasks, I found that quite remarkably I had lost the appetite for work, my motivation gone. I have never done a day's work since, and I always say to people approaching retirement that they should simply take a prolonged break to get the work ethic out of them. Playing golf on the Costa del Sol helps, but you have to have some interests to fill your day. I did a lot of reading and started to take a keen interest in European history, things I had never been able to do before because I had been so focused on my career. Pat and I enjoyed our first long winter break so much that we decided to winter away in future, and realised that retirement above all gives you the freedom to go places and do things that the discipline and restrictions of working do not allow. I had reached all my career objectives, so there was no yearning to carry on working, and I truly felt sorry for some of my friends who remained so focused on work.

So began a new phase of our lives. We bought an apartment in Estepona and lived a life which many of our friends envied, spending summer in Claverley, wintering in Spain and making other trips abroad, maybe spending 50 per cent of the year living in Spain.

Friends used to say to me, 'Don't you miss the seasons in England?', to which I replied that I much preferred to be beside the Mediterranean and enjoying the Spanish way of life and their friendly street culture. We also travelled widely around the country, seeing their great historical cities and reflecting on the time when Spain was a world leader. They had made great strides in recent years, creating the best motorway network and being the first country in Europe to have a nationwide high-speed rail network covering over 2000 miles (when we had only 80), making more motor cars than we did and developing the largest agricultural industry in Europe, and for a nation of only 40 million people they were really on the front foot again. Just 40 years earlier, Spain had been seen as virtually a banana republic where you couldn't drink the water, and the quickest way to get from Estepona to Malaga was by sea.

Spain of course did not take part in the Second World War because it had had its own civil war in the 1930s, a war largely influenced by the Russian communists and Bolsheviks who attempted to install a similar regime in Spain. In the early stages there was a purge of the intellectuals and an attempt to rid the country of the influence of the Catholic Church on the population. Spain, like Italy, had always been a strongly Catholic country, and when the Vatican heard of the murders of hundreds of its priests the Pope came down on the side of the Nationalists against the Republicans and encouraged Franco to fight the Republicans and the Russians, who were now supplying arms and aircraft to the Republicans. Franco secured aircraft and guns from the Germans and Italians, who hated communism and were not prepared to let Spain become a satellite of the Soviet Union. So a very bloody war began, lasting four years, and atrocities were carried out by both the Republicans and the Franco-backed Nationalists. Quite amazingly, many years later when the Germans had taken over most of Western Europe, Hitler expected a payback from Franco, but he and the Spanish people remained neutral in the Second World War. They did not allow the Germans to occupy Gibraltar, which was a pivotal base for the Royal Navy and the gateway to the Mediterranean.

Quite often when I am walking along the beach at Estepona I look out across the Mediterranean and think what it must have been like during the Second World War when the Royal Navy was pitted against the Italians and Germans. Had Franco not allowed us to keep control of the approaches from Gibraltar, the war in the Western Desert would have gone quite differently. As it was we managed to keep control of the Med. Franco always gets a bad press from the British these days, but then lots of people have no sense of history. Franco was on our side and helped the Allies greatly.

Pat's father, who was in the Royal Navy, had his ship blown up while serving in the area and spent several days in an open boat before being rescued. Bruce Arundale, one of my former bosses, was a naval officer, had many close calls while in charge of a flotilla of motor torpedo boats searching for enemy submarines in the area around Malta. He was only 22 at the time and was decorated for his exploits. It was amazing how some people came back from the war and just got on with their lives as civilians – no post-traumatic stress counselling for them.

Spain today is still dominated by Catholicism, and its religious festivals continue to bring millions of people onto the streets across the country. Having dallied with the Muslim religion several hundred years ago when the Moors controlled large parts of the country, it does not, unlike the UK and other northern European countries, consider itself to have a multi-cultural society. Its culture is very much that of a European nation with its Christian Catholic religion still influencing ordinary people. Stalin got it wrong all those years ago when he tried to turn Spain into a secular communist country. It is a peaceful place with friendly people, and I have hardly ever seen a violent act during all the time I have spent there. That is why so many northern Europeans like living there, together of course with year-round temperate weather and excellent food.

Soon after I had bought a house in Spain, an elderly gentleman said to me that he had never regretted buying a home out there. He said, 'You just live longer'. I remember seeing he and his wife grow old together – he lived until he was 93 years old and his wife to 98.

It seemed Pat and I had got everything we had wanted from life. We had our dual English-Spanish life well established, and we had planned our way ahead together. After all, we had virtually spent a lifetime in love, comfortable in each other's company and not really needing anyone else.

However we enjoyed a good social life, especially in Spain, where we had many Continental friends, Dutch, Belgian, Swiss, French and so on; in fact Alcazaba Beach is full of European residents who seem to be able to break down national barriers. We had more friends in Spain than we did in England, and Pat often said that if she had to make a choice between the two, she would opt to live in Spain. Not speaking Spanish fluently was not a problem, as all our friends spoke good English, especially the Dutch – in Holland today most children speak three languages by the time they are 12 years old.

Our Continental friends were certainly an interesting set of people. You could write a book about the residents of the 300 or so apartments ranging from two bedrooms to six which made up Alcazaba Beach. Most of our friends were of a similar age to ourselves and remembered the deprivation they had suffered during the Second World War when their countries were occupied by the Germans, the Dutch particularly having to send their agricultural produce to Germany, so for long periods of the year they existed on milk and eating bulbs. A Belgian whose family had made shoes for three generations during the war said the Germans had commandeered all their leather for walking boots and long leather coats for their army, and throughout the remainder of the war they had used old rubber tyres to make shoes for the Belgian people and keep the business going. When talking of the war years, they thought the English were lucky as we never knew what it was like to live for years under an army of occupation and to have your town bombed and shelled relentlessly. A Polish man said that for the English the war lasted five years, but for him it had lasted 50 years until the foreign soldiers finally went away and their wives and daughters could start to live normal lives. I suppose they were right, comparatively speaking, and talking to these people certainly helped to broaden the mind. However these people, mostly from northern Europe, had worked hard throughout their lives and earned their lives in the sun, playing golf and enjoying the company of their Mediterranean cousins, and we looked forward each year to meeting up with them again.

It seemed that this lifestyle was too good to last, because in February 2007 we had the dreadful news that Pat had a cancer. To start with we couldn't believe it, for at the age of 67 she was extremely healthy. At the time she was using the swimming pool each day and was very fit. One Sunday morning in January she said she had felt some hardening in her left breast, but she didn't think it was serious as she had had a similar feeling some 20 years before which had come to nothing. But the moment I heard this, I called a doctor, who was with us within half an hour. After a quick examination he said he would arrange for her to see a cancer specialist at 10 o'clock on the Monday morning. A biopsy was done and three days later were told she had a malignant tumour.

We travelled back home across Spain immediately for a private consultation with an English cancer specialist at the Priory Hospital in Birmingham. He removed the tumour the following week, but nobody yet realised how serious the situation was. We thought she would get over the operation and continue with life as many friends and relations had, but six weeks later the biopsy revealed the true position. On that fateful day we were told she had a triple negative cancer, one that no drugs could treat effectively. It was a terrific shock to hear this, as only one in a hundred breast cancer patients had this type of cancer. She faced up to it bravely, but I'm afraid it was the beginning of the end.

Paul suggested, and I agreed (not informing Pat), that we should get a second opinion, and this we did, from the foremost specialist in London. Unfortunately his written report agreed with the earlier diagnosis, but Paul and I kept this information to ourselves.

Over the next two years there seemed to be endless treatments, and we were always waiting in the hope of some good news. Pat was subjected to many operations as the cancer moved around her body, including two at a London clinic to remove tumours from her spine. They were very painful for her to endure, and Pat was the bravest person I've ever known. We were maybe thinking she would get better or some wonder drug would come along – we never gave up on life until the very end.

Before Pat died on December 23 2009 we did have a couple of pleasant interludes, including a few days in the best hotel in Llandudno. She had by then been in a wheelchair for some six months. She enjoyed being pushed along the prom and dining in the hotel in the evenings, although she had little appetite for food. We also went to

London for a few days to stay at the Cavendish Hotel in Mayfair. I had used this hotel over the years when visiting the capital and I knew I would be able to wheel her along Piccadilly to see the sights and visit nearby Fortnum and Masons. Her eyes lit up when she saw the pre-Christmas decorations in all their glory and we had afternoon tea in their restaurant. In the evening we went to see *Phantom of the Opera* at Her Majesty's Theatre in the Haymarket. I was pushing her in the wheelchair I had borrowed from the hotel, and the theatre management allowed us to go in through the stage door and park the wheelchair while we sat in the front row of the stalls. She had seen the show some twenty years before and it was her choice to see it again. Knowing she had terminal cancer, the Cavendish went out of their way to attend to her every need, and she enjoyed her short stay in London.

When we returned home I visited a local hospice in case we needed it at short notice, although I knew she wanted to stay at home in Claverley. She deteriorated quite quickly in the following weeks and nurses visited daily. But the cancer had got into her spinal cord and was moving up towards her brain. When lying in bed one evening she started having convulsions which turned into a fit. I was quite helpless, but fortunately one of her good friends in the village was able to come immediately to the house and she gave her a heavy injection of morphine and told me to get an ambulance. When the medics arrived they gave her more sedation and oxygen to help her breathing. After several minutes they carried her downstairs and Jill travelled in the ambulance with them. I was left to clear the place up. I then followed them into Wolverhampton.

By two o'clock in the morning she had recovered somewhat and we were able to have a conversation. Oddly enough she could not remember the events of a few hours before, but she was never to return home again.

By now it was becoming clear to us that there would be no recovery, and I don't think either of us wanted to discuss the future. She was now having heavy doses of morphine and slept for long periods in the day while I just stayed by her to have conversation when she awoke. For the first time in my life I felt I was in a situation that I could not influence, and very much feared the coming days.

Then something happened which I have since described to many people as some kind of miracle. I have to say that Pat had secretly prayed for a release from her suffering. Because there had been no release she had lost her faith in a caring God, and when our vicar asked if he could see her in hospital she at first declined. In those last two weeks she had met an ethnic West Indian who was a pastor at the local church. His wife was in the same ward as Pat, also suffering from terminal cancer. When I was not with her he often spoke to her and prayed for her. In a very gentle way he brought her back into the Christian faith. To cut a long story short, this humble, gentle pastor convinced her that there was life after death and there was a Heaven for all who believed. Quite remarkable, this man made my life and hers bearable during the last days of her life. It was indeed a miracle.

One of the last things she said to me was that I must continue to go to Alcazaba Beach, and I did, but it was never the same without her.

CHAPTER 8

TRAVELLING SOLO

———✦———

Since Pat's death I have travelled quite widely, visiting the Middle East, Far East, India and Asia. I went to India because it had always fascinated me, but I did not like seeing the abject poverty there. I remember taking a bus ride into Bombay and when I got off the bus I nearly trod on the small children living with their parents on the pavement. They had no homes and just lived on the streets, yet hardly twenty yards away across the street was a Bentley car showroom selling cars at £200,000 – what a contrast. I quickly realised why cows are considered sacred and virtually live with their owners and are given food and drink to preserve their lives – it is because they provide the family and their friends with 30 or more pints of milk a day, without which many children would surely die from starvation, and in cold weather their bodies provide warmth at night.

In the communal areas of Bombay and other cities there are dogs everywhere, and they bunch up together and seem to be asleep all day. You are warned not to touch them because they are mostly rabid. I asked an Indian man what the dogs had for food and he replied that they become very much alive at night and kill the rats – without the dogs the rats would overrun the city.

We were told not to use the beaches because they were covered with effluent and the smell was awful, even from a distance. In fact when I arrived by ship I could smell India before I arrived, and it had to be washed down at the quayside. I didn't eat or drink much while I was there. Yet despite the extreme poverty the women in their movement and demeanour showed a kind of supreme confidence, always wearing long dresses even when travelling side-saddle on motorbikes. It was the same with the women picking cotton in the fields in Sri Lanka, a place where some of our party nearly came to grief when the water buffaloes working in the paddy fields stampeded. These animals had massive wide hooves and could very easily trample people underfoot. I was told the wide hooves had evolved to stop them sinking into the mud when working all day in the paddy fields. It appeared that the Sri Lankans thought themselves a cut above the Indians, because they were not so poor.

During my career I had got to know many Indians back home in the UK, and was very impressed by these bright and talented people. Laht was a young man, probably twenty years younger than me, whose family lived in the Manchester area. He was the father figure of the family and seemed to keep an eye on the business interests of his brothers as well as his own. The family had come to the country from Uganda some years before as a result of the expulsion of Indians by the tyrant Idi Amin. Indians are great survivors and Laht knew how to make things happen. The family soon developed away from their shop businesses and moved into other activities. I became involved with Laht when he bought a Dutch wine importing business called Siebrand UK. As I was managing a bonded warehouse he asked if I could give him space in it for his imported wine, and so began a relationship which continued for many years, through good and bad times for both of us. The bad times first came for me when I was made redundant. Laht was doing very well at the time, and when he heard of my misfortune he invited me to travel up to Manchester, where he offered me a job looking after his wine business in the West Midlands. He was a thoroughly nice guy.

What terrible news it was therefore when five years later, after I had joined Cert, I heard that he had committed suicide. Apparently, although he was a qualified accountant, he had expanded far too rapidly and his empire had fallen apart. His brothers were affected by his bankruptcy and were also in financial difficulties. I was told that in the Indian culture, when such things happen, it is customary for the father of the family to take responsibility and make the ultimate sacrifice. His death had a profound effect on me at the time.

On a lighter note, again while I was living in Wolverhampton, one Saturday evening we decided to have dinner at an Indian restaurant, and we were advised by friends to go to a particular one located on what one might describe as the posher side of the city. I hadn't taken much notice of the other clients dining with us, but the ladies in particular seemed to be well-heeled. I asked the waiter for the wine list, and on thumbing through it I found that there was not much below the £20 mark. I was astounded to see towards the back of the list wines costing up to £500 per bottle, such as Château Lafite and Château Petrus, among the most expensive of all wines. Curiosity and I had a word with the waiter, asking him if such expensive wines were always in stock. He said there was a continuous demand for them and whispered in my ear, 'Most of the diners in here tonight are multi-millionaires, sir'. I did hear some time later that Wolverhampton has more Indian millionaires than any other city in England.

King Edward School had a large proportion of ethnic Indian pupils, and I met a lot of their parents, many of them professional people, at social events while Paul was attending the school. Indians do place their great emphasis on their children's education and we were always pleased to welcome his friends and their parents to Claverley. They jealously safeguard their race and background, and I believe they would by no means welcome a daughter of their family getting involved with a white Englishman.

I had a fleeting acquaintance with another Indian when Pat was in the last days of her illness. She was a young oncologist, and she proved to be kindness personified during the final days. She suggested that if Pat liked music, perhaps I could bring in some of her favourite recordings for her to listen to. She explained that I had to understand that although Pat could not speak, her hearing was not impaired and she would appreciate hearing her favourite music. I talked to this doctor many times, and she told me about her family life and her children. She also talked quite openly about her arranged marriage and said that people tended to develop a loving relationship as time went by. She went on to say that most Indian marriages were still arranged, and I was surprised to hear that although she was a professional person, she believed in the tradition. She also commented that with the very large divorce rate and the many broken families in England, it was difficult to convince them that our approach to marriage was better than theirs. That doctor was a very special person.

Burma was the place where the difference in standard of living between rich and poor was most marked, although the ladies masked this by wearing their saris with great dignity, and in fact they did most of the work, as seems to be the case in most parts of the world I have visited. In Rangoon only the main streets are tarmacked and all the side streets are just cut out of the earth with no drains and no sewerage, so you can imagine what the place looks like when it rains. The shacks they live in are built on stilts four feet above the ground to keep the water away from their living space, which is usually one large room. In the daytime it is the living and eating area and at night everyone sleeps there, perhaps the parents and six children all together. When I went into one of these houses I was amazed to see a cobra lying just a few feet from where I was standing. The housekeeper assured me it was a pet and did not attack humans – at night it patrolled the bedroom killing off rats as they tried to enter from below. Strange world, but as I say to people, if you want to see the real world you should travel by sea or overland, because when you go by air you always see the best of things.

Burma is a beautiful country. We travelled up to the 'Road to Mandalay' of World War Two fame and on our return to Rangoon we spent an evening at a hotel in the diplomatic sector of the city. This was where all the rich people lived, and it was very swish and modern.

Whilst there I was told that Burma is the largest producer of teak in the world, but sadly the forests are pillaged by the Chinese and I saw boatloads of tree trunks being loaded and shipped off to China, to end up on the high streets of European cities, having been made into quality furniture.

We then sailed down to Sumatra through the Strait of Malacca, the main shipping channel between the Indian Ocean and the Pacific and the busiest sea channel in the world. Then it was down to Singapore and on to Hong Kong, both OK in their own way but not for me. They say Singapore is the cleanest city in the world, but I saw it a little differently. One morning I stayed on the ship all morning and sat with a G&T looking down at the shipping below. I noticed several small boats, like tug boats, passing constantly. I asked one of the ship's crew, who was doing some painting nearby, what they were doing and he said these were known as the 'bum boats'. Apparently Singapore does not have enough land to deal with sewage treatment, so effluent is piped to the dockside and put in large plastic containers, which are then taken out to sea to be discharged. So much for Singapore's reputation for being squeaky clean.

I think one view of India and the other places will be enough for me. Europe's civilisation and history are much more interesting. I suppose this is because I am European and Christian and can more easily relate to it, and of course it is much closer to home. In fact over the past few years I have visited more than 25 countries in Europe, many of them during a one-month bus tour when I joined a study group to the Balkans on the twentieth anniversary of the ending of the war there. If you are English you have to be very careful what you say when visiting some of the states newly formed from what used to be Yugoslavia. As with so many of the world's trouble spots, the mixing of cultures causes problems which cannot be easily solved, if at all, and trying to mix the Slavs with Muslims created a problem in Serbia and other Balkan countries which will never be resolved. The Serbs still regard Kosovo as part of Serbia and will never recognise it as a separate country because Muslims came into the country from Albania and elsewhere, and in that small part of southern Serbia they became the majority, bringing with them a different culture. Nor is it recognised by the Spanish, or the Russians, who dislike breakaway states. Tony Blair was one of the first leaders to recognise Kosovo, but even today the Serbians in Belgrade would not welcome him into their country, as they see him as the man most responsible for the break-up of Greater Serbia and the introduction of an alien culture into their country.

It was fascinating travelling towards the east of Europe and repeatedly crossing the Danube until it reached its delta on the Black Sea. It passes through five or six capital cities as it flows east and I could see why they call it 'the mighty river of Europe', as it is considerably more so than the Rhine, which beforehand I had considered more important. I have travelled overland up to the Baltic Sea and seen how pathetically destitute the Russians and the Ukrainians who live out in the country are, hundreds of miles from the metropolitan cities, which enjoy a standard of living nearer to that of Western Europe.

I just happened to be in Prague on the anniversary of the Czech uprising of 1968, when students and the people took over part of the city from the communists and put barricades across Wenceslas Square. Three days later the Russians took retribution with tanks, killing over 300 people. It is not surprising that in modern-day Prague the Communist Party is illegal.

Whilst talking about Europe, I would like to dwell for a moment on Switzerland. They say 'You can't have your cake and eat it', but the Swiss have been doing exactly this for many years. Their so-called neutrality, with the country being place strategically in the centre of Europe, has given them the highest per capita standard of living in the world. I well remember being in a shopping mall on the outskirts of Geneva. For the mid-morning break they didn't just serve tea and coffee – caviar and champagne was always readily available, and I simply followed the trend; it appeared to be as normal to them as drawing breath.

Clever people, the Swiss. They will lend money to anyone who wants to fight a war (Hitler included) but always keep out of it themselves. With its low tax regime, Switzerland provides a home for all kinds of malcontents and hypocrites – as long as they are rich, of course.

I well remember on one occasion being entertained by some Swiss people at a very posh place, the Hotel du Lac at Lausanne on the shores of Lake Geneva, where you were served only vintage champagne and the rooms were well above London prices. I noticed a plaque on the wall mentioning Charlie Chaplin. I questioned my host about this and he explained that the dining room had been named the Chaplin Room. Chaplin had been thrown out of America by the McCarthy Commission after the Second World War for being a communist and a Stalinist sympathiser, and he ended up in Switzerland, living in this hotel in the lap of luxury for years. I had to admit that the food was excellent and the views across the lake were stunning.

Another very rich couple, Richard Burton and Elizabeth Taylor, had escaped to Switzerland to avoid paying the high tax rates in the UK at the time, and they too lived in great luxury in a house near Geneva. Occasionally I dined in a luxurious countryside restaurant, and after noticing photos of the Burtons there I asked the barman about them. He told me it was their regular watering hole and rather graciously told me I had been sitting next to their favourite table. Burton was known to have left-wing sympathies, but like Chaplin and many others, he loved the high life in the richest country in the world.

Some time after I retired, the Blair government brought forward a Bill to Parliament which had at its centre a plan to develop regional airports throughout the

UK. It was to be piloted through the Commons by John Prescott, the Minister of Transport, the man who thirty years before had been a barman on cruise liners – his role as a shop steward had caused chaos within his industry.

It so happened that close to the village of Claverley, where we lived, was a former Royal Air Force airfield called Halfpenny Green. Along with hundreds of other Second World War RAF bases it should long since have been returned to agricultural land, but because of some oversight by the county council this ruling had not been followed and this little airfield had continued for the past fifty years or so to be used by recreational weekend flying enthusiasts. Later it had come under the control of a company that wanted to extend its use and renamed it Wolverhampton Business Airport. Despite this it was hardly used, and only by small propeller-driven aircraft. However, in response to John Prescott's air transport plan, things changed very rapidly and the owners put forward grandiose plans to turn Halfpenny Green into a feeder airport for Birmingham Airport and Manchester Airport, and also to fly jet planes to Spain and other parts of Europe, with passenger numbers building up to 10 million passengers a year. This was a startling development which would involve the creation of new and extended runways and large terminal buildings, along with a complete rehash of the local infrastructure to accommodate the people who would be using the new airport.

When this plan became known, people in rural Shropshire were aghast at the prospect of such a massive development, and quite soon an action group was set up to fight the plans. It so happened that a recently-retired managing director of the British Steel Corporation, Peter Cooke, had bought a large country house with twenty acres or so of land just a couple of miles from site, and he was very quickly appointed chairman of the action group, and brought a team together. Because it was known that I had been in the transport business and had been a member of the Chartered Institute of Transport, the body that aims to fit all aspects of transport to the national need, I was charged with the responsibility of corresponding with Government departments, the Civil Aviation Authority and so on.

Peter said at the outset that we need to raise money for a fighting fund. I remember attending a fund-raising event at a local manor house called Dallicote Hall, which was owned by a well-heeled husband-and-wife business team. He was the owner of Charles Tyrwhitt, the London-based luxury shirt makers. His wife was even better known as the owner of the White Company, which had an array of shops. I attended a cheese and wine evening along with a hundred or so invited guests. In the large drawing room there were many White Company settees and I sat on one next to a slightly younger man who introduced himself as Robert Plant and said he had a house just across the Severn at Bridgnorth. He said he was worried that his home would be under the flight path to the intended airport. Not being into rock music, I didn't realise that this man was the world-famous lead singer of Led Zeppelin!

With such eminent company around we quickly had access to the funds we needed and began a wide publicity campaign within a fifteen-mile radius of Halfpenny Green. Streamers, flyers and letters were produced and distributed by a huge team of devotees of our cause, and we held public meetings in east Shropshire and parts of Staffordshire and Worcestershire. We had to fight Wolverhampton Borough Council, the CBI and the local Chamber of Commerce, who were all in favour of the airport, as were some of the Conservative Party organisations, but fortunately our local MP for Ludlow was a Liberal Democrat, Matthew Green, and he fought tooth and nail against the proposed airport and fully represented our case in the House of Commons. I crossed swords verbally and in writing with our Conservative MEP, Philip Bradburn, who supported the airport plan.

I was instrumental in recruiting the man who had the greatest impact on our efforts. A 'green' sympathiser, he was the organiser of a protest and lobbying group called Transport 2000. I had come into conflict with this guy when I was on the committee of the Freight Transport Association, a lobby group fighting for the Road Haulage Association and others, and we were constantly in conflict with Transport 2000. I knew this man rather well and knew he had recently been successful in stopping the extension of flights from Manchester Airport over the Cheshire countryside. I said to this committee that I was aware that this guy was fundamentally against any extension of air travel (he always travelled by rail) and said I thought I could persuade him to join us in fighting the new airport plan. This I did, and one weekend I collected him from Wolverhampton railway station and the whole committee met him at a discreetly-arranged hotel, where he briefed us on the way forward. We couldn't have had a better man on our side. He knew his way around Westminster and the corridors of power and had contacts in the Department of Transport and the civil service, and most important of all, the other groups lobbying against John Prescott's Bill. After nearly three years of protests, the Bill was defeated and the grandiose plans for the new Wolverhampton Airport were abandoned, to the great relief of the people of Claverley and elsewhere.

Many of the older Conservative MPs remember John Prescott as a former barman, and years later when he was deputising for Tony Blair during Question Time in the House of Commons they would barrack him across the House by mischievously saying things like 'Mine's a gin and tonic, John'. He wasn't the brightest of men, and I think he had a pretty thick skin.

After Pat's death I found life in Claverley very lonely. In truth we had only lived there all those years because it was an ideal location for my various jobs. None of my family lived there, so I decided to relocate towards the south, where most of my relations live, and settled in the Oxfordshire town of Thame, which turned out to be an excellent location. I constantly use Luton Airport for the trips to Spain which I make several times each year, and in my eighties I still play golf two or three times a week.

As I bring this story to an end, I have to say that I have been fortunate in having very good health throughout my life. A pity it was not the same for Pat, who had to endure so many operations for one reason or another throughout her married life. I often wonder what life would have been like if our two little girls had survived all those years ago, but I do have plenty of nephews and nieces and their children to occupy my mind. I do think

I have been lucky in meeting so many interesting people, and yes, I have dined with royalty.

When I was MD of Cert we annually took a table at the Wines & Spirits Benevolent Society Dinner at the Grosvenor Hotel in London's Park Lane. Among his many duties the Duke of Edinburgh was a patron of the society, and one year we were sponsoring the top table where the Duke would be sitting. I remember that when he left his car he was virtually swept across the few yards of pavement into the hotel – obviously security against the risk of attack by potential assassins was of prime importance. He dined with us for a couple of hours, making lots of small talk, and then soon after the loyal toast he was swept out of the hotel as quickly as he had arrived and returned to the waiting car and his bodyguards. I have a lingering memory of how slim and fit he looked for about a seventy-year-old, but I noticed that his dinner jacket looked as if it was thirty years old and was very old-fashioned – it could well have been the oldest suit in the Grosvenor that night. Clearly he was not interested in being a trendsetter any more. It was a little different from years before when I had seen him as a young man at a polo match in Cheshire. He rode about in a convertible Alvis Six sports car and was very good looking, dashing and debonair. He was staying with naval colleagues in a big house in Cuddington.

On another occasion I sat with Peter Foden, the MD of ERF Trucks, at a lunch celebrating the opening of a new regional service for one of their distributors. I was invited because I had recently placed an order for twenty trucks to add to the Cert fleet. The Duke of Kent was the guest of honour and was to perform the opening ceremony. I sat opposite him at a table for eight people for a couple of hours and found him to be a thoroughly nice guy who did not at all dominate the conversation, something the Duke of Edinburgh did tend to do, but then the Duke is a very different character. A step up the royal ladder, so to speak.

Once on a cruise liner I met a chap who had played a real part in history. He was a retired Swedish diplomat, and while cruising I had dinner with him most nights as we were both travelling alone. During a long career as a diplomat he had been his country's ambassador in several capitals, but he said his most memorable role was at the time a peace treaty was signed at the end of the Korean War. Because Sweden was considered to be a neutral nation the Swedes brokered the peace deal which ended and the war, and he was present at the historic signing ceremony which took place in the demilitarised zone on the border between North and South Korea.

The former Swedish Ambassador was quite an intelligent individual with a ready sense of humour, explaining that the purpose of his trip was to reacquaint himself with Far Eastern territories he been located at years before. It didn't seem to recommend diplomacy as a career for a young man as he had 'lost' three wives somewhere along the way. This trip lasted for nearly thirty days and as two single chaps travelling alone, we became good friends and I looked forward to our evening chats. After all, we were a couple of guys with wonderful futures behind us, as they say!

A LAST WORD – THE STATE OF THE NATION

My life occupied a good part of the 20th century and into the 21st. Children of my age group entered a world in which Great Britain, although just an island off the European continent, was by far the most influential nation in the world apart from a growing America, its empire controlling over a third of global nations, and I suppose we British were pretty smug about all that power and influence. But things were beginning to crumble. In the Far East, and particularly on the Indian sub-continent, the effect of Bismarck's creation of Germany in the 1860s, where a bringing together of former regional powers, ie Prussia and Bavaria, created potentially a political force of great strength. Hitherto we had only had to deal with France, Spain and other less powerful nations. The Franco-Prussian War of the 19th century held no fear for us, but a warlike emerging Germany was a different matter altogether.

If Bismarck had never been born, then perhaps the First and Second World Wars would never have taken place. Also if Bavaria had joined the Austro-Hungarian Empire instead of Germany, things would have been different, but Bismarck's influence was crucial. Anyway, although we had no part in starting either world war, we simply honoured treaties with the Belgians and the Polish, so we got deeply involved, and that, more than anything else, led to the demise of Great Britain.

As an aside, it is interesting to note that it was always the French who had been our traditional foe in Europe and our more friendly relations with the Germanic race were largely sustained during the Victorian years. However, and rather tragically, in the two world wars which followed it was the British who actually declared war on the Germans. How sad that in a little over a hundred years, when Britain reigned supreme in Regency and Victorian times, we emerged from the Second World War heavily in debt, with a crumbling empire. Our reign as top dog was over and the Americans took over our international role.

Nevertheless, when I was in my mid-twenties, Britain still produced some 15% of the world's steel and manufactured over a million motor cars a year, and 90% of the cars running on our roads were produced in England. But economically, things were not looking good. The Attlee government's policy of more nationalisation took as its beacon Russian communism, whereas America and the now burgeoning post-war economics of Germany and Japan retained the philosophy of the enterprise system. However just a few years later when Macmillan took over, we had a decade of real prosperity and he managed to build over 500,000 houses per year for several years, using British tradesmen – that was over 50 years ago. Now we are struggling to build 250,000 houses a year. Additionally, looking back 50 years or so, our manufacturing industry was 80% of our GDP. Now it is below 10% and still falling. We may have won the war, but we've certainly lost the peace to our European neighbours.

Maybe it's a matter of our best brains being pointed in the wrong direction by our educationalists. I remember going to an annual speech day and prizegiving at King Edward's School, Birmingham, in 1980, where the Chief Master, Fisher, made a very appealing speech telling parents to persuade their children to read science and engineering when they went up to university, not, as he put it, the comfortable and soft options of medicine, law and accountancy. But I'm afraid his words fell on deaf ears – only six out of 80 studied science or engineering. That's an example of how the British have lost their search for inventiveness. When there are much more comfortable and less hazardous careers on offer. Nearly all the many worthwhile inventions over the past 40 years have been made by the Americans, the Chinese, the Japanese or the Germans. They have a more focused approach on what a nation needs to be successful, and their governments look after their wealth.

Reluctantly I have now concluded that the present voting system is wrong. I believe our first-past-the-post political system is at the root of our problems. The electorate flip-flops from left to right because of our highly confrontational two-party political system – ten years in one direction, followed by ten years in the opposite direction is the way it has been throughout my life. The successful nations, like the Dutch and Germans, do things quite differently, constantly entering into coalition politics, avoiding massive changes of direction.

I think sometimes we should shut down Westminster for ten years and let the Civil Service take over with the plethora of laws we already have. They are the professionals who run the country. The politicians are just a bunch of amateurs at best. If we had an interregnum for 10 years a Royal Commission of Enquiry could come up with a better system.

In concluding this summary, what has led to our ever-decreasing economic and political influence compared to those former years of glory is the quite shameful lack of political leadership. Shame we didn't have a Konrad Adenauer, the creator of the German miracle after the Second World War, when paradoxically we in Britain came out of that war with a country and an industrial base which were largely intact.

Most of our substantial companies are now foreign-owned. Basic industries have been allowed to be sold off with the consent of successive British governments. As an example, virtually all the freight and passenger-carrying vehicles are powered by engines from abroad. During my lifetime, so much has been invested in the NHS and the Welfare State that there has been no money left to build up our industrial base – if it hadn't been for people in the City of London paying as much income tax as Birmingham, Liverpool, Manchester etc put together, we would have been sunk years ago. Yes, the city generates 25% of our GDP.

I sometimes wonder what our great inventors, men

like James Watt, Abraham Darby, Thomas Telford and George Stevenson, who powered the British Industrial Revolution, would think of the comparative state of our industry today. We still have great universities, but they are being used increasingly to educate students from China, India and wherever. We still have good British brains, but the past fifty years tell us that that early promise has not been followed by achievement and performance in industrial terms.

It is often suggested by politicians that we are the fifth largest economy in the world. In reality, without the City of London we are probably down to number ten or so in industrial terms. Rather sadly, we are a nation on real decline, and a significant part of that decline has taken place on my watch.

Finally, from a personal position and one which has been a guiding light when making decisions throughout my life, I adopted a simple motto when making such judgements, taking long experience into consideration: that it is better to be roughly right than precisely wrong. Maybe the so-called experts should bear this in mind.

BV - #0057 - 231120 - C12 - 203/127/13 - PB - 9781861519573 - Gloss Lamination